Wild Harmonies

Wild Harmonies

A LIFE OF MUSIC AND WOLVES

Hélène Grimaud

Translated by Ellen Hinsey

RIVERHEAD BOOKS

a member of Penguin Group (USA) Inc.

New York 2006

RIVERHEAD BOOKS
Published by the Penguin Group
Penguin Group (USA) Inc., 375 Hudson Street, New York, New York 10014, USA •
Penguin Group (Canada), 90 Eglinton Avenue East, Suite 700, Toronto, Ontario
M4P 2Y3, Canada (a division of Pearson Penguin Canada Inc.) • Penguin Books Ltd,
80 Strand, London WC2R 0RL, England • Penguin Ireland, 25 St Stephen's Green,
Dublin 2, Ireland (a division of Penguin Books Ltd) • Penguin Group (Australia),
250 Camberwell Road, Camberwell, Victoria 3124, Australia (a division of Pearson
Australia Group Pty Ltd) • Penguin Books India Pvt Ltd, 11 Community Centre,
Panchsheel Park, New Delhi–110 017, India • Penguin Group (NZ), Cnr Airborne
and Rosedale Roads, Albany, Auckland 1310, New Zealand (a division of Pearson
New Zealand Ltd) • Penguin Books (South Africa) (Pty) Ltd, 24 Sturdee Avenue,
Rosebank, Johannesburg 2196, South Africa

Penguin Books Ltd, Registered Offices: 80 Strand, London WC2R 0RL, England

Library of Congress Cataloging-in-Publication Date

Grimaud, Hélène, date.
 [Variations sauvages. English]
 Wild harmonies : a life of music and wolves / Hélène Grimaud ; translated by Ellen Hinsey.
  p. cm.
 Translation of: Variations sauvages
 ISBN-13: 978-1-59448-927-3
 ISBN-10: 1-59448-927-0
 1. Grimaud, Hélène, date. 2. Pianists—France—Biography. 3. Wolves. I. Hinsey, Ellen, date.
II. Title.
 ML417.G73A3 2006   2006023105
 786.2092—dc22
 [B]

Printed in the United States of America
10 9 8 7 6 5 4 3 2 1

Book design by Meighan Cavanaugh

Wild Harmonies

One

I have no nostalgia at all for childhood. Throughout the passing years, I have never had the feeling of a paradise lost, but rather of a paradise to be found, elsewhere, one that was waiting.

A paradise inside me, buried.

"She's never satisfied!"

As a small child, I heard these words a thousand times, spoken by those who looked at me, looked after me, and discussed me. Long before I understood what the words meant, I made them into a family, much like my stuffed animals. Their family name was "Un." They were the "Uns," and each of them had the same ability to put a surprised or worried look on my mother's face. Alone in my room, I would repeat them to myself, separating out what I remembered of their syllables. I created a family tree for them. The great-grandfather of the words (I actually had a great-grandfather, whom I adored) was Uncontrollable. There was no great-grandmother—there was no point, since I didn't have one myself. (By the way, I thought I was fairly unique in this respect: my few inquiries at school confirmed just what a treasure I had— not one of what my parents and the teacher called my "little schoolmates" was blessed with a great-grandparent.)

After Uncontrollable, there came quite often Unsatisfied. Then Unmanageable. Or Impossible. Undisciplined. Insatiable. Insubordinate . . . Unadaptable. Unpredictable.

"Make her play some sports."

No doubt someone had diagnosed an excessive amount of energy, an overabundance of vitality that could be released through martial arts or tennis. I did both; I took dance as well, but I was found to be completely unfit. What I hated about ballet was not just the physical discipline: the costume disgusted me too. Nothing about it pleased me, not the leotard, the tutu, the slippers, or the pink satin. I looked appallingly like the dolls that, on several unfortunate occasions, were given to me at Christmas. I furiously smashed them all against the wall. The very idea that someone would think of giving me such a thing horrified me. Imagine how I felt about looking like one!

I take a certain pleasure in practicing martial arts, and I played tennis regularly with my father—lovely shared moments with the one whose Cartesian spirit, rigor, and appreciation for order and schedule were so troubled by my restlessness, my unpredictable moods, and my sudden passions.

When he caught me in one of those moods, I could feel that he was upset. It was that same distress I learned to measure in the intense dilation of my mother's pupils when she discovered, once again, what I had been up to. With the best parental intentions in the world, they tried to find an outlet for my insane behavior. But nothing could hold back the energy that I turned on myself. Nothing could bring me closer to other children. I had no playmates, either at school—which was an ordeal—or during after-school activities that were suggested to me.

"Look at this drawing."

The teacher displayed a large piece of paper on which my mother could make out only a series of squares. A teacher herself, she was well acquainted with every kind of behavior, but she fell right into the trap: "I don't understand what it is."

"It's very simple," the teacher said, sighing. "Like all the other children, Hélène was asked to draw chickens in a barnyard. Your daughter has scrawled a picture of wire mesh. This is very disturbing."

There followed a series of whispers between them; the "Un" family tumbled from their lips. Advice. The inevitable frowns.

"Is it true that you refuse to play with the others during recess? Don't tell me that in the entire school, there isn't one single boy or girl who meets with your approval . . ."

My mother was always worrying. I rubbed my cheek against her hand. She had a very distinct scent, a mixture of lavender and chalk, often with a hint of garlic that soap couldn't entirely remove. Garlic from Provence that witnessed my birth, garlic that my mother would sprinkle on dishes like so many tiny white pebbles in an aromatic forest, all the while singing old Italian songs for me. I hated the fact that she worried. The frown that dug a valley just above her nose struck me to the heart. I experienced horrible feelings of guilt. I felt mean. And yet the meanness wasn't me. Not me in essence. While I threw those dolls against the wall—crushing the affectionate gesture of the giver along with them—it wasn't me. It was something in me that wanted to get out, to express itself, to escape.

"Mama, what's a limit?"

"Something that marks an ending."

"So my body is my limit, then?"

My hateful limit, which something in me sought to throw out the window. Mean? Children were mean sometimes. I could close my eyes and relive the meanness in their laughter and the secret blows they rained on their scapegoat during recess or the kicks they aimed at the flank of a sick dog. How could I explain to her the aversion I had for the others, the way they stayed in packs, in groups, striking out and targeting the weakest? I thought they were pathetic. I felt completely different from them. And I was . . . wasn't I?

"Nanou, you mustn't ask in a loud voice why the concierge for the building walks like a duck. He limps because he's crippled, and he heard you. That upset him, and you shouldn't hurt people. It's cruel."

I was three years old. The next day we ran into our concierge at the same location, and I exclaimed: "You see, Mama? I didn't say that man walks like a duck. "

I don't remember my mother's reaction to these words. I only recall the instantaneous response: the concierge's visible sorrow struck me to the heart. I felt it physically. It was mixed with sadness, because the little girl he had known since birth had succumbed to the cruelty of tactlessness, the power to hurt.

I remember being horrified by my own words, and I remember

as well my remorse and suffering. It had the metallic taste of the schoolyard, the same deep purple discharge as when I watched my classmates mocking someone, when I saw their aggressiveness—especially the boys'—always in a gang, always pushing one another and fighting. And yet, if I had had to choose sides, I would have chosen theirs. Better than anyone, I could pick out the best branches for climbing a tree. I could have beaten them all at climbing, running, and playing tag. I liked their marbles best of all: hands hovering over shooters, that choreography of fingers—by turns powerful and delicate—that created a fascinating ballet beneath the sun, which lit up in dazzling flashes the colors of the aggies, the cat's eyes, the rainbows and opalescents. I liked everything about marbles, even their music—the light tinkling they made in pockets, the dull ring that signaled victory when they knocked together. But, for whatever reason, games and girls didn't go together. You had to use your body when playing marbles, and not be afraid of crouching and bending. And girls were always on their guard with their gestures; their movements were constrained. The girls took care not to wrinkle their skirts or let their socks get twisted around their ankles, while the boys treated their clothes with disdain, staining and ripping them without a care, with an arrogance that fascinated me.

For all that, I didn't "feel like a boy": I was a child, and I was appalled when just because of my sex I was expected to behave in a way that was predetermined, conventional, and completely at odds with my nature. Happily, my mother respected who I was, and she never tried to force me to wear skirts, blouses, or smocked dresses.

During recess, to avoid the others, I would run and hide in a classroom or in the corridor, behind the coats hung on their metal hooks. Sometimes a supervisor would find me and send me back out into the schoolyard. I had my spot, in the corner of a high wall that protected my back. There, motionless as a lizard, I would observe everything that was going on, especially the older fifth-graders.

There, always accompanied by two or three other girls, Sabine would stroll under the chestnut trees, as nonchalant as a queen. I envied the laughter and the bonds among those older children, that strange atmosphere woven from the secrets that they shared and that put a blush in their cheeks. Sabine was very tall with round cheeks, and there was something very soft in her appearance and very direct in her smile. There was something almost Madonna-like about her. I loved the movement of her hair on her shoulders when she walked and, most of all, the way she had of silencing all the noise around her—the cacophony of an entire schoolyard—whenever she appeared. She suspended sound. I was in awe of her. When I thought about her, I was suddenly seized by a sharp, burning impatience to grow up. I felt anew the desire to leave my body, to throw my limbs in all directions—that feeling that ejected me from the world with the strength of a joyous sob.

I didn't get on any better with my classmates in the schoolroom. My teachers failed to keep me in line. Not that I was a bad pupil, it was just that I interrupted all the time, and I daydreamed when I should have been paying attention. I asked inappropriate questions; I was constantly overflowing with words. I couldn't feel entirely blameless about the remarks that rained down on me. I was gnawed by guilt and for a long time, at night, in my dreams, I would feel the howling mistral wind blow me off the enormous school stairway, which, in my nightmare, had neither banister nor anything to hold on to, and I would be lost in a dizzying fall. I would wake unharmed, of course, shaking and sweating—amazed to find myself in my own bed, as if the fall should have sent me into another dimension, a different kind of elsewhere, where I would finally feel at home. Beyond me. Greater than me, I didn't know where, but this desire for another place was in my being, even though it was a lack. It was a pressing need, and this inexpressible presence, its ineffable absence, tormented and haunted me.

In 1532 in Aix-en-Provence, the town where I was born, the president of the Parliament, Barthélemy de Chasseneuz, published a collection of his legal opinions, most of which had to do with "common proceedings against pernicious animals." Apparently, he himself had defended, with a skillful plea, the rats that had invaded the town of Autun. In this collection, and without the least trace of humor, Chasseneuz drew up a list of the common questions raised by the misdeeds of pernicious animals, which he names: rats, field mice and water voles, weevils, slugs, June bugs, caterpillars, and other vermin—all of them harmful devourers of crops.

Chasseneuz asks if they should be brought to justice, and then proceeds to compile a list of case law in effect at the time. The jurisprudence is categorical: Animals must be brought before a court to which they have been summoned. If they fail to appear, a lawyer will be appointed to represent them. These cases were examined exclusively in the bishop's courts; the sentences that were handed down extradited pests and vermin from the cultivated lands that they devastated but, in recognition of their natural and legitimate need to feed themselves, authorized them to take up residence in uncultivated fields. If the accused pests did not comply, which none of them did, the judge anathematized or excommunicated them. Flies and field mice in Laon were excommunicated, much like grasshoppers in Troyes, along with caterpillars and wild rabbits.

And yet not all of the members of the animal race that committed crimes were excommunicated. Domestic animals were also tried in due form, but before a lay court. These animals—pigs, cows, donkeys, dogs, and horses—having been found guilty of ruining shops and gardens, stealing food, or refusing to work, or much more seriously, of murder, were arrested and taken to prison, where they awaited their sentences.

Just as they would for any other criminal, the police drew up a list of charges, carried out an inquiry, summoned witnesses, and took their testimony. The verdict was handed down. The sentence was pronounced and finally read out to the guilty animal in its cell. In Normandy in 1386, a sow that had been condemned to death was dressed as a man from snout to tail, then dragged by a mare (oh, dishonorable treatment) to the town fairgrounds for execution. In front of the Viscount de Falaise and his peasants assembled with all of their pigs (the better to enlighten them) and the sow's owner, placed in the first row "to cause him shame," the executioner sliced off the sow's snout and slashed one of its thighs. Then he slipped a mask of a human face over the beast's mutilated muzzle and hung it by its hind legs until death ensued, after which the sow was burned at the stake.

What had the sow done to deserve such a death, with its fellow creatures gathered to witness the spectacle of its execution? It had gotten into the house and eaten the arm and half the face of a three-month-old baby, Jean le Maux, who lay sleeping in his cradle, and who died of his wounds.

In the same way, at Gisors, an ox was hung for its crimes; at Clermont-en-Beauvaisis, an ass was shot for kicking its new mistress; and at Baugé, a ewe and its owner were hung, then burned together in a sack for bestiality. There was no shortage of animal trials, but it was the pigs that were the stars of the chronicles of the animal criminal trials, which were commonplace up until the seventeenth century. At that time, pigs would wander freely through town and countryside, where they served as road menders and garbage collectors, and tore up cemeteries in order to get at the corpses. In 1457, under questioning, another sow in Savigny-sur-Étang in Burgundy, admitted (*sic*) to having killed and, along with her six piglets, partially eaten five-year-old Jehan Martin.

Why these trials? Quite simply so that animals, whose nature had not been clearly defined—did they have a soul or not, and what was its essence?—could have the benefit of a judgment and a just and equitable treatment. Like any human being.

Sometimes I was completely happy, as when my parents would suddenly decide to get away from our house in Aix. The idea would seize them all at once: "Shall we go?" "Let's go."

No more school, no more neighbors, no more glances in my direction. All restrictions were left on the doorstep. Each one settled into his or her own corner, shoulders relaxed, guard down. During these little trips—generally over a weekend or during short school holidays—I truly felt I was finally present. I was me, indivisible, an actress in the moment—no longer marginalized, or watching with a sharp eye what was happening around me, events in which I could never manage to participate. Hiding exhausted me and at the same time it filled me with a stormlike electricity, as if the electrons of the universe were coming apart, churning my blood, my bad blood, my rebellious blood. But where did that blood come from?

There in the car, the gentle, infinite rhythm of travel rested on me like a bird's wing, an invisible cloak woven from the wind by the hand of an angel. I was transported, in every sense of the word. The silence formed a cross: inside, the horizontal purring of the motor; outside, the vertical shrillness of the cicadas . . . I fixed my gaze on the mountains, on the pass of the nearest hill where the horizon intersected with the road and I waited, in complete faith, in a calm and peaceful impatience, convinced that at that exact point the face of God would appear to me.

He didn't reveal Himself? I waited for the next hillside to appear, the final turn in the road, on and on, without any lessening of my optimism or my certainty that the rendezvous would happen. I played endless rounds of hide-and-seek with God.

For a long time, I thought that I would discover Him behind Mont Sainte-Victoire, where my parents loved to roam. For this reason, the faraway mountain always seemed magical, but once I drew near, once its proximity gave the lie to the possibility of this planned encounter with the Lord, I didn't like it at all. In the same way we say someone looks out of sorts, I thought it looked "out of climate."

I thought it looked wrinkled, lined by too many fields, scarred by too many roads, power lines, telephone poles, cluttered by too many villages. To me it seemed shrunken and asphyxiated, the Scarface of mountains.

"Look at Mont Sainte-Victoire, Nanou . . ." my mother would begin, wanting to depict it for me in all its glory. Paul Cézanne painted endless versions of it. He lived in Aix until his death, and at the end of his life he never stopped saying, "No one will get their hooks into me."

My mother never missed a chance to teach me, to sow seeds of wisdom. In her treasure trove of knowledge, the paintings of Paul Cézanne were held in high esteem, but her preference was for Italy, where (via Corsica) her family came from. She and my father both taught this musical language, so full of mystery to my ears. When they exchanged secrets in my presence, when they voiced their concerns about me, my parents spoke Italian. My ears thus contained a motley fugue of words, whose similarity to French sometimes gave me a limited insight into their discussion, like a performance glimpsed through a keyhole, partial and off limits. It was thanks to Italian that I learned, for the first time, that despite all the love they have for you, one could be an enigma to one's parents. And to the others who are closest to you. For this reason, Italian will always remain for me the language not only of masquerades and carnivals, but also of truths glimpsed from afar. Maybe it is for this reason that I caught early on my mother's passion for Pirandello. I found in his plays a reflection of the same sort of split personality from which I continually suffered: a distancing not from myself but from the world. It was the art of withdrawal, of retreat.

Nevertheless, there was one place where I did not have this feeling of strangeness. It was in the Camargue, and it was magical. A dream that emanated from the sea. . . . Just a few hours away by car, one plunged into another universe, a place where something wild and untamed prevailed. Once past Arles, when we took the Route des Salins or the Route des Saintes-Maries, my attention became as taut as a bowstring. My heart beat faster as I searched the horizon with all my might, waiting for the dirt road that would take us into the secret recesses of the delta.

Even though everywhere else I felt like a wrong note, here I was a part of a vast harmony. In the ponds and pools of water stretching out to infinity, one felt the strength of the Rhône; one understood how it could become a bull, charging straight ahead and darting from side to side. This was no longer the sun of bees and mimosa in the garden, but the merciless dazzle of a midday that came from everywhere at once. Flamingoes and wild horses stirred up a powerful perfume of salt and soil. The freedom with which the birds would suddenly take flight and the horses would gallop away, shaking their manes, nourished my soul. The Camargue was more than a landscape—it was a brief glimpse, a dazzling intuition of a harmony between my soul and what was to come. There, for the first time, I had the premonition of great things, of my destiny.

I knew I was in another kind of territory, one of those spaces from which one could soar, and nothing gave me greater pleasure than being there. I ran completely joyful, completely exuberant, through this land of horizons where everything is excessive: the sun too cruel, the wind too strong, the waters too unpredictable. I repeated the words of Paul Cézanne: "No one will get their hooks into me." Certainly, the Camargue taught me as much, and sometimes I stopped leaping and running, stopped rolling in the tall grass and made myself walk on tiptoe so as not to disturb anything. I was a guest, merely tolerated, and I was reminded of this by my sunburned shoulders and my mosquito bites; at the same time, I was horse, wind, raging tide, soft hyacinth. I rolled in the waves. Finally at peace with my body, I was neither girl nor boy. I was simply, completely, and marvelously alive.

Although Philippe de Beaumanoir asserted in the thirteenth century that beasts had no knowledge of either good or evil, as late as the sixteenth century many jurists, including Jean Duret and Pierre Ayrault, thought that animals that had committed murder or infanticide should be punished by hanging or garroting. After all, didn't it state in the Bible that animals that had committed homicide should be killed because they were guilty and impure? "If an ox gore a man or a woman, that they die: then the ox shall be surely stoned, and his flesh shall not be eaten; but the owner of the ox shall be quit" (Exodus 21:28).

In the Middle Ages, animals were considered to be partially responsible for their acts because, like all living things, they possessed a soul. This soul was vegetative like plants, sensory like the simplest animals, but intellective as well, like the soul of man. Did it also have a rational and a spiritual component? Medieval scholars also debated whether animals rose from the dead, if there was a special heaven that was reserved for them, and if, on earth, they should be treated as morally responsible beings. Don't laugh—the question is a serious one, and indicative of a praiseworthy era when the fate of animals and the respect owed to them—even if this was in reference to the danger that they sometimes presented—were solemnly pondered and studied. After all, as Saint Paul says, all creatures are "children of God." All except the serpent, which the Lord condemned for its criminal collusion with Satan in the Garden of Eden.

Except the serpent for God . . . and the wolf for man.

Considered to be a scourge as soon as its presence is spotted in the countryside, the wolf has been hunted down for thousands of years. Hunting parties are organized to flush it out. Wolves have been blamed for every evil, every crime (how many infanticides have been attributed to them?), and every disappearance (how many rapes and murders have been covered up by blaming wolves?). They have been accused of pure witchcraft—lycanthropy, the most heinous crime of all. Wolves convicted of this crime were drawn and quartered, and then burned alive at the stake.

What is lycanthropy? The spell with which a man or a woman

changed into a wolf—when it was not Satan himself who took on the wolf's shape, hide, red mouth, and yellow eyes, opening the gates of Hell in the heart of a peaceful countryside.

Unfortunately, this bizarre fantasy and the martyrdom that ensued for wolves do not date back only to the Middle Ages. They are as old as time.

As old as antiquity, when, according to Pausanius, Zeus punished King Lycaon of Arcadia for having sacrificed a newborn baby on an altar. The leader of the gods changed the king into a wolf for ten years. It was the ultimate punishment.

Wolves have been hated since the Middle Ages, when doctors diagnosed a very particular physiological illness, also called lycanthropy. This "wolf madness" aroused lust and sexual frenzy in pretty, young women, who howled at the moon, showing their breasts to the stars, offering up their sex—a soul-devouring sex.

❧

I had no real friends, and no brother or sister. I didn't complain. My parents supplied me with everything that my imagination needed. With books, first and foremost.

As soon as I returned home from school, I threw myself into my books, shoulders firmly propped up on my pillow, schoolbag forgotten under my desk. I had my favorites and my waiting lists. They were summoned to speak with me. I could start two books at the same time: I would pluck one like a daisy, page after page, or sample it like a petit-four. The other I would devour at once, greedily, without a crumb of displeasure. My passion for books carried me along like a cloud, from the moment I bent the corner of a page to mark my place, to the following day when I returned from school. The friendship offered by their characters protected me against the inanity of the schoolyard and the boredom of the classroom. Alexandre Dumas watched over those childhood years with unparalleled generosity, consideration, and care for my pleasure. Such elegance! Such a wealth of description so that I would never get lost in a thinly defined setting! Such ingeniously constructed plots! Impatiently, feverishly, I waited to find out how things would turn out. While I read, my thumb stroked the edges of the pages, whose thickness promised dozens of other secret rendezvous. *The Count of Monte Cristo, The Three Musketeers, The Vicomte de Bragelonne* . . .

Sometimes I mixed the stories up a little bit. D'Artagnan paced up and down in the Château d'If. Milady sailed down the Volga. I was with Queen Tamar in the mountains of Georgia. I think it is to Dumas that I owe my attraction to big books, which later drew me to Tolstoy and, above all, Dostoyevsky. But my first book, my first love affair with literature, was the Bible.

I read it inside out and back to front. I opened it at random. Certain chapter headings fascinated me: "Wisdom of God Revealed in the Plagues He Visited upon Egypt," "God Teaches His Children by the Punishments He Inflicts on His Enemies" . . . This made for a potent brew; I didn't know the full list of ingredients, but the blend of essences—"wisdom" and "plagues," and "teaches by punishments"—created a growing turmoil in me, incomprehensible but powerful. The names mentioned and the places cited were also magic: Aaron, Shalmaneser, Pekahiah, Remaliah. The trials to which God submitted his people satisfied my mysticism. I was thrilled by this tempestuous notion of love. I delighted in reading stories that I thought were particularly daring, and sometimes I was astonished that my parents put this book within my reach: murder, trickery, infanticide, incest . . . It was infinitely more exciting than the rubbish my teachers droned on about in catechism class, where I was terrifically bored.

I really liked the God of the Old Testament, and I fervently prayed for Him to appear to me. From my reading, I had deduced that such a revelation would necessarily take place on a mountain, and I ended up believing that mountains had been specifically created for this purpose. I was less captivated by the New Testament. The Gospels seemed pretty washed out compared with the Song of Songs and the prophecies of Isaiah, certain passages of which I read until my head swam: "And it shall be an habitation of dragons, a court for owls. The wild beasts of the desert shall also meet with the wild beasts of the island, and the satyr shall cry to his fellow; the screech owl also shall rest there, and find for herself a place of rest" (Isaiah 34:13–14).

Hyenas and satyrs. Jackals and owls. What a fantastical bestiary those night hags rode! Even the Camargue itself, an incredible place of skies and secret places, didn't harbor any of that menagerie—not even a gentle unicorn, even though it was pale and had a mane like the beautiful white horses I loved to watch. And even though I loved Jesus, I thought he was a bit cold toward animals. Why didn't he invite the birds and fish to hear him preach, like Saint Francis? After all, hadn't the peaceful ox and the gentle ass watched over him at his birth?

I let my book fall. I dreamed. In my room, interminable and

delicious spaces of boredom unfolded, those empty hours that my parents did not fill with either after-school activities or television. As I look back, I understand the privilege of those moments when I could practically feel my bones growing. In the slowness of the dream and the thickness of the silence, one could measure the density of the time that flowed past. The hours of boredom of childhood are gardens of time, tilled with frustrations, worked over with slow eternities, haunted by far-off futures . . . I wandered among them, a prisoner of my room and of winter Wednesdays. There I hatched desires and images. I defined myself, learned myself by heart, and, above all, I drew up endless escape plans.

When I played this game, my innate sense of drama and my predilection for the tragic led very quickly to the worst scenarios. Thus, chronically angry at the world, I sank into images of revenge that stung my eyes with tears—the most delicious of all was that of my own death, and I inflicted it on the others with delectation. Oh, how they would regret their severity and their comments! Their inflexibility! Oh, the remorse that would gnaw at their souls! How they would regret not giving me the dog that I had longed for so much. Regret having taken the side of the headmistress, who— when she saw that I had sneaked into school a puppy I had found in the street, for the whole school to adopt as a mascot—had, without further ado, taken the dog to the humane society.

I placed my lifeless body in a thousand places where they would never expect to find it. Then, as in the movies, I made all the expressions of terror go across their faces: stupefaction, incredulousness, horror, outrage . . . Too bad for them, they had deserved it. So I stayed dead and refused to come back to life. But what if my daydreaming really did cause my death? Chilled to the bone, I banished the images at once and locked my brain to keep them from coming back. To distract myself, I threw myself into my books. It was no use: my fantasies had surely set in motion the destructive, pitiless wheel of fate. Everyone knew it—or at any rate I did, knew it in my bones—imposing one's desires turns them into truths, or worse, realities.

My parents were out. Why hadn't they come home yet? I paced up and down my room. I pressed my face to the window and contemplated the rainy landscape and the halo that my breath made on the glass. Waiting for their return, I listened intently to the noises of the house.

The empty house became extremely talkative. The tick, tock of the clock in the kitchen, the abrupt awakening of the refrigerator, the creaking of the furniture. I checked the clock a thousand times. They really were late. Impossible. My father was never late. His military precision was legendary. They must have had an accident. It was my fault! I was an orphan. The poisonous images from my daydreams came back to haunt me. There I was, in tears, dressed in black, in complete despair. Cosette, Cinderella—all the orphans of the world lined up for the casting call. My guilt continued to grow until—at last, at last!—I heard the door open.

"Nanou?"

Ah! The voice of my mother immediately checking that I was there, that I was all right. The wave of panic retreated from my heart. With a huge sigh, I threw myself on my bed. The mercury descended in my veins, and my lungs expelled a gust of funerary chrysanthemums.

My mother was singing old Italian songs. While I read, I listened to the bustle in the kitchen where she was preparing supper. Her magic hands created whole symphonies: the tomtom of the knife on the cutting board as she chopped garlic and vegetables, the muffled cymbals of the onions sizzling in the pan, the kettledrums of the pots as they banged together.

Once again, it was the best of all possible worlds. My mother was home and suddenly the idle, wandering seconds and minutes— lost in dizzying spaces where time faltered—once again formed their divisions and battalions, sixty seconds to the minute, sixty minutes to the hour, in a measured, regular rhythm. Tick-tock, eight o'clock, the echo of the evening news on the television, the murmuring of lives in the building, and all of it, inside the circle of the clock face, stood at attention once more and followed the orders of the big hand and the little hand. Armor-plated, unassailable, rustproof time, time slowly stirred by an affectionate mother, time under the close surveillance of armies of clocks— had returned.

When my mother finally called me to the table, I left my room with a spring in my step, in a wonderful mood, my heart overflowing with love and compassion. Seized by an irrepressible elation, I spun around on the tiled floor, I hung on my mother's neck, I kissed her, and leaped some more, which invariably made my mother say to my father that really, I was quite an exhausting child. . . .

In northern Germany, it was strictly forbidden to say the word "wolf" during the twelve days of deepest winter. The time of the wolf, *die Wolfzeit*, is also bathed in a black sun. It is exactly at this time that Sköll and Hati, the two black wolves of the forces of evil, are on the prowl seeking to devour the sun. In the twelfth century, Bartholomew the Englishman asserted that the wolf was a terrible beast that lived only on toads and that, like Attila the Hun, it scorched the earth permanently wherever it walked. Gaston Phébus, in the fourteenth century, stated that the wolf had a predilection for human flesh, particularly that of infants—the most tender of delicacies.

In fact, only one single culture has respected the wolf, and even then only in mythology, because in real life it hunted the wolf mercilessly for its pelt. The legends of the Celtic and Scandinavian lands—with their endless winter nights and their crystalline-pure skies in the white rhapsody of the North—made the wolf a symbol of light. Whereas others made the wolf howl at the moon, for them the wolf was the incarnation of the sun. There in the heart of those huge spaces, gripped in their blinding truth by the cold, in that other Eden, that pre-Adam paradise where neither lie nor pretense flourished—in the Great North that permitted no respite, no languishing except in love—the wolf was life itself, more biting than the frost. Life itself, with an incredible intensity.

As far away as Russia and its far-off steppes, the wolf appeared: mythic, bringing good fortune to the kind, the weak, and the persecuted. Who, with unswerving faithfulness, saved the young Ivan Tsarevitch from certain death, dishonor, and disenchantment? The great gray wolf of *The Firebird*.

You don't know the story?

Every night, the golden apples of Tsar Demian were stolen, despite a watchful guard and high walls built to protect his garden of rare flowers and precious trees. Furious at this thievery, the tsar promised his kingdom to whoever caught the criminal. The tsar's three sons took up the challenge. One after the other, they kept watch at night, but only the youngest, Ivan Tsarevitch, managed to stay awake. He discovered the thief: a firebird! He pounced on the bird, but only managed to grab hold of one feather.

The sight of this feather aroused the king's envy. He wanted to save his apples, but now he also wanted this marvelous bird. I will give my kingdom, he declared, to the one who brings it to me.

No sooner said than done! His three sons went off in search of the firebird, each astride his horse. Who would reward the courage and the innocence of young Ivan? A great gray wolf took him on its back. With stubborn loyalty and unspeakable self-sacrifice, blind to the disobedience of the young Tsarevitch, who imperiled the success of the venture at every turn, the wolf led him to his goal. He ran and ran, leaping over mountains in a bound, crossing valleys in a single stride, his paws devouring the distance while his tail erased his tracks! He led Ivan first to the firebird, then to the horse with the golden mane, and then to the beautiful Princess Hélène. And back again . . .

Aha! you say to yourself—Hélène and the wolf. So that's where the connection began! Well, no. As the story of the firebird says, a tale is short in the telling, but a deed is long in the doing. I met the firebird and the gray wolf much later, thanks to Stravinsky, who composed for them.

I met them after music had entered my life. After Alawa, the she-wolf with glowing eyes, crossed my path on a road in Florida. She, too, saved my life. But wait, we're not there yet.

Did I tell you? My mother is Corsican. Of Italian and North African descent, yes, but Corsican. She left the Island of Beauty to continue her studies on the European mainland—which, to her young eyes, consisted entirely of Aix-en-Provence. In Corsica, she lived in a little mountain village, Olmo, and for the first several years of my life, we spent our summers a few kilometers from there, on the coast at Ghisonaccia. It is to Corsica that I owe my first memory. I am incapable of describing this place in any real detail or the landscape in such a way as to direct someone from A to B. When I'm alone, I love the game of unwinding memories like a lazy snail, of imagining a landscape in which I can wander in memory's golden light. But the images I have of that place stand out, like an island lost in a nocturnal sea, or rather, like a phosphorescent spring glowing in terra incognita. I have no memory, or very little, of the journey by boat to set foot on that maternal land, or the road, or the house where we stayed. After I started the piano, we never went back.

Nevertheless, my memory contains precise fragments always brought back by the particular, unforgettable perfume of that land—a mixture of scrub brush and wild grasses, of sugar and pungent flowers, a blend that sometimes reemerges by chance, during a walk or, strangely, in a kitchen. And then behind my eyelids a very detailed landscape emerges, one that has never left me. I remember very clearly a path in the mountains at the center of other paths where, leaping nervously, goats would cross; I remember the mystery of their oblong pupils in their yellow eyes and the scree of little pebbles beneath their gray, pointed hooves. An ash-colored donkey pushes out his lower jaw, stretches his neck with all his might, and lets out that incredible cry, the noise of a saw, a cry of protest, almost of pain; that cry cradled my nights and my play in that place.

My greatest joy was to go into the maquis in search of donkeys and goats, to discover, in the dry grass, the tiny luminous black beads of small rabbit droppings, to spy out the quivering V of their ears, like two Indian feathers, sticking out above a shrub when the sound of my steps surprised them, and then to see them dash off, their pace punctuated at intervals by the comma of their white tail. I loved dissolving into that landscape. Crouching down, all ears. Waiting for who knows what, amid the screeching of the cicadas. Sniffing the earth for a moment, convincing myself of my own existence by the warm odor of my own body, which I checked, and which I inhaled, my nose buried in the neck of my sweater. This is the clearest memory of all.

I have only vague impressions of walks in the cool of the evening under the chestnut trees of the main street of Olmo, trailing in the footsteps of my mother. Are they even my memories? I don't know if my imagination reconstructed them from the words of my parents, if I made up the image of those massive, incredibly tall and austere houses, or the smile of that ancient woman dressed completely in black, or the silhouettes of the gnarled old folk, twisted like grapevines, sitting on benches in front of their

doors. But I remember vividly the pain of the cut I received deep
in my heel. The pain—and the joy—of my first injury.

How did it happen? Impossible to remember. Stupidly, no
doubt. Where did it happen? On the beach, whose shape—except
for a fragment cut from time—I do not recall. Was it wide? Long?
Curved? Once again, I don't remember. There was simply a muffled burst in the fleshy part of my heel and blood that ran out.
The gash was a deep one. It was decided that I would have to be
stitched up. The only doctor in the village—even though he had
what was necessary to cauterize the wound—had no anesthetic to
ease the pain of the needle entering the thickness of the skin or
that of the passage of the thread pulled through ten times. My father was pale. My mother clenched her teeth.

"Don't look."

My foot was soaking in an enamel basin filled with a purple,
vaguely fluorescent liquid. Like tiny ocean sponges, the froth of
my blood expanded in pale pink ripples.

"Hold her tightly."

They dried my foot, over which now leaned the face of the
doctor. My breathing touched him. He frowned in concentration.
He was so close to me that I had the impression I was seeing him
through a magnifying glass. The wrinkles of his forehead made a
series of S shapes, like waves in a naive drawing. Floating above his
shoulder, my father's face, deathly pale. And then nothing more.

No more images, only the memory of what I felt, and felt
intensely.

"Hélène? Hélène? Are you all right? She looks so strange."

I jumped. Completely absorbed by the discovery of this new

sensation, I had forgotten my parents and their concern, which was exacerbated by my expression. . . . Instead of screaming as they had expected, instead of struggling, crying, and throwing myself into one of those fits of hysterics that only I knew how to throw—the last one I would inflict on my family concerned the puppy that I had been forbidden to adopt at school—I was smiling. A sweet smile, a smile of ecstasy, nourished by each plunge of the needle into my flesh. How can I describe that feeling? Then again, can you put pleasure and pain into words? Can you even recall those sensations and relive them in the same way that you experienced them? You abstractly recall that you felt pain; you don't remember concretely how you felt that pain. Thus, I can't concretely describe what I felt in that small doctor's office, lost in the middle of a Corsican village. I remember that I was not suffering. On the contrary, I was delighted.

It was not the happiness of a kiss from my mother, or the pleasure of petting my great-grandfather's dog, or of cradling our neighbors' puppy in Aix, the puppy I would walk in the evenings. No, it was not that type of pleasure. It was an intense but separate pleasure, not due to an external cause but born in me, of me, since a part of my body was the source. It was a joy at the outer edge of suffering, and this pleasure cast a strange—and, I would say, intensely satisfying—spell on me.

"Hélène?"

I understood that my smile was frightening them. I got hold of myself, grimaced, and pretended to clench my teeth.

"She's a courageous one for her age, this little one," said the doctor as he continued to treat me. "She's six years old? Bravo."

I understood that what I had glimpsed three years earlier was true. For the second time in my short life, I realized I had lost my innocence.

The first time was during Christmas. I had found a stuffed animal under the tree—exactly what I had wanted. It was a very cuddly panther that I immediately named Bigaro. I loved stuffed animals—I collected them. I had a whole family, and perhaps to compensate for his systematic refusal each birthday, name-day, and Christmas to get me a puppy—claiming that dogs were not made to live in apartments—my father concocted an elaborate staging for my toys while I was away at school. I would leave them lined up on my bed in the morning. When I returned home in the afternoon, I would find them on the balcony or in the living room. The bear would be by the honey-pot, the cats in front of the television, and the mice would be having a picnic.

The Christmas I discovered Bigaro, I showed my happiness in the way I knew how: with excess, scenes, and exuberance. As a result of my jumping, I discovered that the tiled floor of the living room was extremely slippery. I lay on my stomach and spun around like mad, just for the pleasure of sliding.

"Look how happy she is with her present!"

My parents interpreted my game as an expression of joy. And so, to please them, and only to please them, I prolonged the happiness, continuing to turn while clutching the stuffed panther in my arms. I laughed gleefully until I suddenly understood that something in my life had changed forever: I was pretending.

Once more, that summer afternoon in Ghisonaccia, I gave them my innocence. To hide the nature of my desire from them.

To protect them from me and from the chasms I knew had opened in my soul. I put on a normal expression, accompanied by a little grimace of pain when I put my bandaged foot to the floor, and I squeezed out a few fleeting tears to complete the picture.

A few minutes later, all was forgotten, but it was with that injury that my troubles—all my troubles—began. After that, concern never left my parents' hearts whenever they discovered a new manifestation.

Two

On the night of the full moon, in order to turn into a were-wolf, one must absorb a potion of aconite, opium, and bat's blood that has been prepared in a copper pot. After scrubbing the skin with black soap, the candidate for this transformation paints his or her body with this magic mixture, slowly rubbing every square inch, which is finally covered with the skin of a freshly killed wolf. Then, hands armed with steel claws, one attacks other human beings, eating their flesh so that the metamorphosis is complete.

This witchcraft recipe was no doubt the prelude to the terrifying story of the Beast of Gévaudan and the other, less well-known tales of the Beast of Auxerrois and the Beast of Vivarais.

This last affair (also called the Beast of the Gard or the Beast of the Cévennes) lasted eight years, from 1808 to 1816. The monstrous animal was never killed. Recorded accounts mention its large ears, elongated snout, long bushy tail, and—according to eyewitnesses—long, trailing teats. The Beast killed twenty-two people, including nineteen children under the age of twelve. Six of those killed were decapitated, a strange fact that was also noted in the case of the Beast of Gévaudan. In contrast, the Beast of Vivarais displayed a strange recklessness—it entered houses to devour its victims—and a particular curiosity: it undid the pins used to fasten the undergarments of its female victims.

Without a doubt, the solution to the enigma of these three "beasts" can be found in the affair of Jean Grenier, who stood trial in Bordeaux in 1604. This thirteen-year-old boy from Périgord was accused of having killed and eaten fifty children. He confessed without being pressured or tortured, and even provided many gory details.

What did Jean Grenier say? A man, "the Lord of the Forest," had given him a wolf pelt and had rubbed him with an ointment. Thus, turned into a werewolf at nightfall, the boy began attacking his peers at the edges of forests, in thickets bordering the roadsides. A child would pass by, and Jean would pounce on his victim, stab him to death, and devour his warm, tender flesh.

Nothing would have been known of these crimes, and this dismal story would have been filed under the chapter of mysteries in the footnotes of history if Jean Grenier hadn't fallen in love. His heart grew weak when he discovered—after attacking her in order to devour her—the beauty of Marguerite Poirier. Shaken, he ended up sparing the innocent girl. She immediately ran and reported the assault. Did she reveal the guilty one? No. Proving that belief in werewolves was deeply rooted in the collective imagination, Marguerite Poirier described the creature that had flung itself on her as a huge, monstrous animal with a reddish-brown coat. . . .

The hunt intensified, but in vain. Other children disappeared. Their horrifically mutilated remains were found in thickets and on the sides of wooded paths. Perhaps dozens of other children would have been mysteriously eaten without the truth coming to light, as at Gévaudan, if Jean Grenier had recovered from his lovesickness. But the memory of the young girl—the warmth of her skin in his hands, the palpitations of her young chest under his teeth, the salty taste of her perspiration on his tongue—haunted him. He wanted Marguerite. He wanted her to love him, to admire him. Alas, in the village, she didn't know him or recognize him. On the other hand, the crowd of her admirers never ceased to grow, asking her again and again to tell the story of the attack, demanding new details about the beast's claws, its breath, its eyes and pelt. Marguerite trembled, and Jean Grenier suffocated. So, to seduce the young girl, Jean Grenier ended up boasting to her of his crimes, sure that she would yield in the face of his strength and before the force of a desire mixed with terror.

Alas! Terrified, the girl ran to denounce the monster. Jean Grenier was arrested, brought to trial, and accused of lycanthropy. He was sentenced to spend the rest of his days in a monastery, where the prayers of the monks did not save him from madness: for the rest of his life, he lived on all fours, feeding only on raw meat.

It's strange—when someone asks if I was a happy child, I automatically answer yes. But if I really think about the question, if I plunge back into the memory of who I was then, the answer is a resounding no. Objectively, I had every reason to be happy. But I was suffocating. Not always, and not all the time. To put it simply, my earthly envelope constricted me, the awareness of my envelope, of this me that limited me, and from which I wished to escape. One day, seated at my school desk, concentrating on writing left-handed—which made my neighbor squint—the letters that I was learning, all at once I understood, or rather, all at once I experienced this "me," my me that concentrated all my energy within the limits of my body, even as I longed to burst out of it. I remember feeling the pressure of the entire universe on my skin. It was an incredible, dazzling, overwhelming moment, an experience of my presence in the world that I would remember several seasons later when, for the first time, I encountered the piano—but with the exact opposite sensation.

That first time, at school, I felt closed in, imprisoned. Entirely concentrated on this me, I understood that I was the frontier of the world. And like the young girl in the High Tower, I could only contemplate and never enter the life that spread in all directions— the cosmos and the skies that gave me a premonition of endless nights; fields, mountains, and seas undulating to a horizontal infinity in the same dizzying state; beneath my feet animal burrows, sap, pulsing roots, and the fusing of magma. It was much more than just the points of the compass around, above, and below me. This was a starting point, the big bang of my consciousness that forever afterward has led me to say—especially with regard to music—that each one of us is an act of magic, that we almost never take the wrong path, and that quite often we just haven't gone far enough. After all, what is to come is not so much something to be discovered as invented.

That day at school, I identified for the first time the intense urge to be somewhere else, someplace better, to find the ideal place—as if I had known it previously! I looked out the window at the playground and the plane trees—my hand poised in mid-sentence—fixated on the certainty that I could move my body by my gaze, that my gaze could take me away with it.

This intense need for escape would sometimes be rekindled in the evening, and nearly always in my joy at succumbing to a sort of vertigo. To put myself to sleep, I sought that giddiness, the sensation of weightlessly falling. I had a sudden craving for it, and after dinner, when my parents told me, "Hélène, go to bed, and don't forget to brush your teeth," I concealed a devilish smile. I would throw myself on my bed, turn out the light, and shut my eyes very tightly. Suddenly, a smooth surface the color of *marrons glacés* would appear before me, covered with all sorts of colored dots: blue, mauve, yellow, and green. They were mostly metallic colors. I would focus all of my attention on these luminous dots until finally, slowly, my room began to turn around me. I would slip, slip, until I felt the wonderful sensation of infinite dislocation. I knew that I no longer consisted of anything, that I was outside myself, that my envelope was empty, and that this nothing was all that remained of the world outside myself, and that what remained was all.

For a long time I could fall asleep only by experiencing the vertigo of the void, the slide into nothingness, abandoning myself to

this weightless fall. There was only one other ritual capable of opening the door to space and delivering me from this feeling of oppression. All I had to do was recite, in the darkness, the prayers that
I had learned at catechism class during the day. I started by saying
them to myself in a rhythm that matched the contents, and then I
would drone them until I was exhausted. To tell Jesus that I was with
him with all my heart, and not with the mob that howled for his
death, I convulsively recited the Our Father, followed by a Hail
Mary, in an incantatory rhythm, then by the rosary, then by chaplets, then by series of chaplets, hands clenched and eyes shut, ham-
mering away at the prayers in my bed, in the hope of who knows
what sort of revelation. Thus, the action was transposed into the
rhythm, and the melody carried the thought, radicalizing it.

Several weeks after experiencing the intoxication of this recita-
tion, I began to try to repeat the Hail Mary and the Our Father
for as long as possible, to try to exhaust the notion of infinity. I
set the rhythm and phrasing, three by three—three Hail Marys
followed by three Our Fathers—then seven by seven. When my
diction or intonation did not satisfy me, when I thought I had
erred, fallen short in excellence or in the progression, I started
again from the beginning. I could recite for hours on end before I
was satisfied—it was pathological. Sometimes dawn would find
me exhausted, asleep, except for my lips that continued to move,
forming the words "full of grace," "the Lord is with thee," "now
and at the hour of our death." Really, my lips moved by themselves, animated by this string of syllables, like those paper shapes
that girls make at recess and put on their fingertips.

I don't know now if it was the content of the faith or the rhythm of the prayers that pleased me more, but those recitations marked the beginning of the mental dimension of my musical training. The revelation came from there, from the habit and practice of reciting that saved me from boredom and, no doubt, from failure.

I made the connection several years later. One evening in Paris, the night before the examination at the Conservatory, I was consumed by doubt, unable to practice. I had to learn a piece by Charpentier, a piece that bored me and which my memory refused to register. With this work, my presence in the city and at the Conservatory, as well as my whole future, seemed difficult, vague, drowned in a murky uncertainty. Once again, that old feeling of oppression, of being from elsewhere, had me by the throat, even though I wanted to keep working. But I couldn't—my body and spirit felt leaden, and I could not get over this obstacle.

I ended up going to bed. I wanted to prepare for the certain disaster that awaited me the following day. I closed my eyes, and then suddenly, all at once, the practice of prayer came back to me except that it wasn't "full of grace" that I was reciting, but the entire Charpentier score that I scanned and repeated to myself as I used to repeat the Our Father, until the rhythm and intonation were satisfactory. Prayer had taught me to place before myself, like a performance, in images and colors, all that I needed to absorb.

The following day, I played the piece with brio, total control, and extreme clarity. I understood that to remember is also to invent. Memory is the magic art of composition.

❧

In September 1731, a strange, crouching silhouette caught the attention of a shepherd in Songy. The figure crept from one grapevine to another, hiding behind them. The shepherd approached and discovered with stupefaction a disheveled girl, in the process of skinning frogs, which she ate along with leaves. When he took her hand, the girl offered no resistance. The shepherd led his discovery to the château, and Monsieur d'Épinoy, the Lord of Songy, ordered the shepherd to shelter the girl and to take care of her.

In the weeks that followed, Monsieur d'Épinoy studied the strange creature the shepherd led each day to the grounds of his château. He followed her when she fished for frogs—her preferred form of sustenance—in ponds and ditches, and studied her when she looked for roots in the garden, preferring them to lettuce and sweet peas. Above all, he invited the entire countryside to come and view this new attraction. "One noticed that everything that she ate, she ate raw," an eyewitness reported in the *Mercure de France* of December 9, 1731, "including the rabbits that she skinned with her fingers as skillfully as a cook; one watched her climb trees more easily than the most agile woodsmen, and when she was perched on top, she imitated the songs of the various birds of her country."

She was about eighteen, spoke an incomprehensible mumbo-jumbo, lapped up water like a cow, and refused to eat cooked food, but she was extremely skilled at needlepoint.

This combination of the refined and the savage caused a sensation: the exoticism of this animal-woman caused a stir. For a time, Monsieur d'Épinoy erected a tent to show off his phenomenon. Her fame was such that the Bishop of Châlons became indignant. After all, the young woman was not a talking monkey! She deserved an education, care, and religious training. On October 30, the *intendant* ordered that she be placed in the Hôpital Général in order to completely humanize her. She was baptized Marie-Angélique Memmie. The nuns forbade her to eat raw meat, walk about naked, express herself in grunting noises, or climb trees. However, the walls of the establishment could not keep the legend from spreading. The King and Queen of Poland had heard rumors of the young girl, and so had the archbishop of Vienna. Royalty! They could be neither defied nor denied, and Marie-Angélique was presented to them. In their presence, she skinned a young rabbit and ate it raw, tore off her clothes, and leaped into a ditch, where she wreaked carnage on frogs and wriggling worms.

The Queen of Poland was wild with joy and wrote immediately to her daughter, Marie Leszczynska, wife of Louis XV, commending her to summon this phenomenon herself. No sooner said than done: Marie-Angélique was transferred to a convent on Paris's Left Bank and later, endowed with a modest pension, installed in a small Parisian apartment. There, she was visited by the poet Louis Racine, Lord Monboddo, and the scientist Charles-Marie de la Condamine. Her case was studied. For her, Linnaeus invented an infrahuman species: *Homo ferus* (wild man), just above the orangutan. Lord Monboddo, who had studied Marie-Angélique closely, agreed wholeheartedly: "Orangutans and wild children need only instruction in order to learn speech."

Buffon was delighted with the experiment. Thanks to this "wild, absolutely wild" young woman, "a purely natural state has come to be known."

Marie-Angélique lost her teeth and her hair, and wasted away in her Parisian cubbyhole. However, without knowing it, she nourished the great question of the Enlightenment. Was man naturally good, as Denis Diderot maintained? Or was he, as Racine asserted, good only through refinement and education, but completely wild and vicious in his natural state, corrupted by original sin? The Jansenist poet based his view on the carnivorous—and therefore cannibalistic—impulses of Marie-Angélique, a sort of cavewoman. The Rousseauists seized the debate—Marie-Angélique embodied the legitimacy of their philosophy: a successful education reveals the potential of a fundamentally good nature. The debate continued to rage, while Marie-Angélique continued to grow sickly. She died in total oblivion, supplanted by Victor, the Wild Boy of Aveyron—the other wild child, who even more powerfully dominated people's imaginations.

As for the debate about the goodness of nature or the perversion of education, it went out of fashion. A "religious" reading was completely refuted, and questions of people's relation to education and nature would henceforth be decoded by psychoanalysis. . . .

For example, Sigmund Freud's account of the Wolf Man.

Baudelaire wrote, "Love greatly resembles an application of torture or a surgical operation." At the time I was growing up, I knew nothing of this aphorism, but I lived it. I loved life and the world passionately. I wanted to feel them in my skin as deeply as possible. I experienced this for the first time in Corsica with that little surgical operation, when the doctor sewed up my heel that had been cut by a bottle shard. That delicious pain had made me exist more than anything else in the world, had fit me into a time and a place—it had given me myself. I had gained access to life by giving over my entire being to that injury.

The repetition of the experience was accidental: a fall on a gravel path. My knee burned. The pulp of my flesh appeared underneath drops of blood. I sat down at the edge of the path and contemplated my kneecap, skinned at the hem of my Bermuda shorts. I brought my two knees up under my chin. I squinted in order to observe as closely as possible this part of my body that quivered each time it was brushed by a breath of wind. The wind was dying down? I blew on my skin to intensify the pain. I remember thinking that life itself was rubbing against me, and that I could thus perceive it with a clarity that was particularly sharp, elemental, and significant. And it was magnificent to bear those wounds on my knees and elbows, that geography of brown scabs that boasted, like a medal on a lapel, of unforgettable exploits and an aptitude for childhood adventures: leaps into streams, races down alleyways, skateboard takeoffs and flights into the masts of plane trees. "Boo-boos" flourished on my limbs like so many medals; they were the pride and joy of an age when the world was still territory to be conquered and time was eternally conjugated in the present tense.

I came to love my injuries, to caress my scabs, to slide the tip of my index finger over their convex surfaces, hard and gleaming like the back of a June bug. I loved to lift them delicately, contemplating the tender pink of the skin underneath, and then to pull them off with a swift tug; either the skin started to bleed again ("Oh Nanou, it's going to leave a scar!"), or a small, pale continent was revealed, still sensitive.

I don't know anymore if it was out of a desire for symmetry or from the need to re-create—with the same intensity and pleasure—the wonderful pain of the needle that stitched me up, but I ended up feeling the need to wound the other side of my body, as a way to stay in harmony. I wanted the same constellation of scabs on both knees, the same cuts on my fingers, the same burns on both hands. An injury to one elbow and, like a tightrope walker on his cable, I was deprived of my balancing pole. I lost my equilibrium, my precious equilibrium with the world, my wholeness; my body limped.

This was not some new infatuation: as far back as I can remember, I always felt this need for symmetry around me. Thus, when I cut my right hand, I would immediately gash the left one. A hangnail that stuck out would be ripped out down to the quick, and then I would attack the other hand. I dreamed of fractures. When my mother was out, I would run to the bathroom to wrap my wrists and ankles in Ace bandages.

My room also received the same meticulous attention. On my desk, there had to be the same number of pencils on either side of my books, and my books had to be laid out at the same distance from my notebook.

In my room, as soon as I could move the furniture, I placed my table in the exact center of the wall. I could retie my shoelaces for hours, so that they would be exactly the same, and I tried to find ways to lace them to be sure that, on the first try, the second knot would be identical to the first. Although my desire to inflict myself with artificial stigmata stopped abruptly when I was about thirteen, the mania for symmetry preoccupied me for much longer. When I began to give concerts in foreign countries, I would spend hours rearranging the furniture in my hotel rooms. At home, in my closets, I would endlessly refold my clothes, attempting to conjugate colors and sizes, to decline materials and styles. When I got back after a concert, I avoided turning on the light, sure that the hotel chambermaid had disturbed my intelligent, precious order. In the dark, feeling my way, I moved the ashtray a few centimeters, realigned the desk blotter with the hotel's insignia. Instinctively, with my eyes closed, I turned the base of the television so that it was exactly parallel to the wall and not placed so that I would give myself a stiff neck if I wanted to watch it in bed. No matter how tired I was, I could spend a full hour fussing over the bedroom, the bathroom, the towels, my things laid out on the sink. If I didn't, I could not fall asleep.

And then—was it a sign?—I was saved from this obsession by dolphins. They were on a sweater I was particularly fond of, which I took everywhere. As usual, I had packed it in my suitcase before leaving for a concert tour in Japan. I was staying at the Hotel Takanawa in Tokyo. I was exhausted, and yet, despite my extreme fatigue, I spent more than an hour refolding the sweater, ruler in hand. It had to be perfect, with exactly the same number of dolphins on each side of the fold, with not a millimeter of difference between the right and left sides, and between the top and bottom. My determination began to turn to madness. And then, suddenly—why then?—I opened the window, grabbed the sweater, and threw it out into the void.

According to the medical textbooks, I had been suffering from OCD, obsessive-compulsive disorder.

Much later, I understood that this obsession with the symmetry of things—including the wounds that grieved my parents so much and that my teachers at the schools I attended found so "unhealthy"—simply betrayed a deeper aspiration: the search for equilibrium, an equilibrium of my entire being in the world and in the universe. I was, in fact, seeking my center of gravity, that exact point that belongs to everyone and that defines one's place, beyond all pain and frustration—the place of self-fulfillment.

I needed my compass points, an equal distance between my north and south, my east and west. To find my heaven over my head and my earth beneath my feet—made of what, I didn't yet know—and in each palm, not the stigmata that I dreamed of when my mother told me the story of Padre Pio, from whom the blood sprang like two springs, two fountains of pure joy. No, not these stigmata, but two contradictory, opposite elements, for which I could become the union, the hyphen, the perfect synthesis, the reconciliation.

According to Isaac the Syrian, God created the angels in silence and—poised on the boundary between the spiritual and the material—man. Man who gathers within him all the dimensions of the universe, and for this reason composes the "unique harmony consisting of different sounds." Isaac the Syrian also said that a human being is a cosmic entity; he cannot be separated from this background, but is part of it. And it is the pulsation of this cosmic dimension that explains part of his being.

Sin? We have all sinned. The feeling of having sinned? We have all felt it. That sensation of intense shame that stunts the soul. For me, it was the day my neighbor caught me in the act of hurting myself. I had left the door of my room open. She had noiselessly passed by. She saw me. We exchanged glances. I understood what Eve must have felt when the heavens over Paradise opened so that the wrath of God could be heard, and her overwhelming desire to cover herself, disappear, dissolve. I hid my hand behind my back. She said nothing, but her extreme pallor and her eyes that darted like panic-stricken butterflies struck me to the core.

Despite all my precautions, my mother had discovered my obsessive manias. Obviously, the many bandages that I wrapped around my injuries attracted attention, hers in particular. Although she had openly expressed to me her concern at first—"But it's so odd, Hélène" (and I guessed that "odd" was a good example of an understatement)—afterward, she said nothing. She didn't speak about it, but she never stopped being watchful of me.

And thus began the meetings with my teachers and the enrollments in various activities: dance, judo, tennis. I grew bored with the first two very quickly. Tennis, the final attempt at sports, amused me a bit more, but for all that, neither the self-inflicted wounds nor the obsessive ordering disappeared.

"Perhaps it's an excess of mental rather than physical energy?"

It was my father who first voiced this hypothesis, after all the other developmental attempts had failed.

"What if we were to enroll Hélène in a music class?"

Someone had told him about an introductory music class for very young children, given by Françoise Tarit, in the center of Aix. The next day I was at her house.

Above all else, I loved the place. On the upper floor of one of those old Provençal houses with their austere gentility and blond stones, bathed in the sharp perfume of the plane trees, a large, high-ceilinged room held a single instrument: a piano. It glowed in the gold of that late afternoon, and its reflection rippled gently in the waxed terra-cotta floor tiles. My father spoke to the woman, who from time to time threw me a glance. Then she said to me: "Come and listen."

She sat down at the piano and played a little piece by Schumann. And like the genie that emerged from Aladdin's lamp, a magical atmosphere filled that music salon. As if in a dream, distant feelings stirred in me—or rather they were born in my very depths, my furthest interior. I remember, as if it were yesterday, the enchantment I felt, as though I had been seized by the idea of the infinity that music evokes. I had the physical sensation of an opening, the impression that a path opened in front of me, as if a door had opened in the wall and a luminous, straight path led from it toward a harmonious revelation. I remember breathing deeper, more expansively.

My father agreed to one half-hour lesson per week, with other children. Together, during these beginning sessions, we practiced singing and percussion. Françoise Tarit tested our ear, our sense of rhythm, and, quite simply, our desire for music. At the end of two weeks, when my father came to fetch me one evening, she took him aside.

"Hélène really has a gift. You should have her start playing piano. In my opinion, it could lead somewhere. If you like, I'll give you the address of a professor who prepares students for the Conservatory."

I owe my start in music to my father. My mother balked; she wasn't thrilled by the idea. She was afraid that music would close me off even more, permanently separating me from the company of other children. My father insisted . . . and he won. Two hours later, a rental firm installed an upright piano in our house, and with the address of Jacqueline Courtin in his pocket, my father made an appointment. I was in my seventh year. The adventure had begun.

Music suited me, because, I think, that in order to be a musician, one has to be compulsive. There is an innate compulsion, as in every other activity that requires a search for perfection. I think that all children who play an instrument or practice a sport have this in them. From the outset, one needs to have a certain way of thinking that is practically pathological, and at the same time a certain exuberance, an expressive strength of communication.

I think that it was because of this strength of communication that I loved dogs, all dogs. Ripp, my great-grandfather's gray German shepherd, and Rock, the neighbor's dog. I loved to take Rock for a daily walk, letting him take the lead, pulled along by his red leather leash. He dragged me from one apartment to the next, visiting the residents of our building, mostly old ladies living alone. I saved my last visit for the retired couple and their daughter, all three of them dears. I would come hurtling in, Rock twirling like a top and me, wound up, expansive, hanging from the necks of those three people whom I loved like a second family. Two mad dogs, in fact, whipping up a storm, leaving shimmering trails of phosphorescence in the light that filtered through the shutters.

That evening, when Jacqueline Courtin had agreed to take me as a pupil, I ran to tell them—talking about it prolonged my happiness and kept in check my impatience to push open the gate of my professor's little garden, to pet her large dog that, I think, frightened her a little, and—above all, above everything—to play that instrument.

I started the piano immediately. Playing seemed perfectly natural to me, an extension of myself. Jacqueline Courtin had a very special and very intelligent way of getting us to work. She combined music theory and reading scores with practice. The tactile pleasure of playing, of seeking inside myself the emotion that I never, ever, in any way had been able to express or bring to a peak, this delicious pleasure completely satisfied me. I experienced the simultaneous pleasure of conveying my feelings and of receiving an echo of them through the magic of those black and white keys, of breathing in the presence of something perfect. I had the physical feeling of being a part of the music.

My parents never had to tell me: "Hélène, practice the piano," "Hélène, your scales," "Hélène, time to practice," "Hélène!"

On the contrary, I immediately and completely invested myself in music because music gave me pleasure. That hour-long piano lesson was the summit of my week. I still dreamed of becoming a veterinarian or a lawyer—in order to right wrongs. But with the piano, I went from pleasure to happiness, from discoveries to revelations, from joys to physical sensations of freedom. Thus, one day, I was able to read the études of Chopin and to play some of them. How can I explain the feeling? Those little marks, those forbidding notes on staffs, that mysterious alphabet erected like a wall to circumscribe understanding—all at once they revealed their secret. I held the philosopher's stone that transformed ink and paper into a melodious architecture, a world that was deep, tender, and strong. That day, I physically experienced the word "chord," the chord struck on the piano, the dissymmetry in the arrangement of my hands, which nevertheless generated notes and perfect harmony, lifting me up the rungs of a magnificent order. I brought forth a new verb into the world. I flew.

I was thunderstruck, so happy, that I ran to our neighbors' apartment—"Come quickly, come quickly!"—as if an extraordinary event had just taken place, as if I had lifted a leaf of a cherry tree and found fruit in the form of the nightingale's golden song. They sat around me, serious, amazed, gently nodding their heads despite the mistakes, and they said to me, "That's very beautiful, Hélène." They were my first audience.

I was fully seven years old, the "age of reason," and I had a completely sensual, carnal approach to instruments. It was so strong that on two occasions I preferred the cello to the piano, because that stringed instrument required a total physical embrace; I remember my emotion at the Conservatory at Aix when I saw a little girl bent over her cello, her temple placed against the sound-post, her slender and supple wrist like the stem of a flower, sway-ing with each stroke of the bow, and her fingers on the strings in the key of G. Then I was seized by the cello, and the contact was nearly fatal.

I was fully seven years old, and I entered into the world of music with my intuitive way of understanding: direct communication with what was evident. The clarity of nature, and that of music, both of which can be understood only by allowing them to de-velop internally in their wholeness. Intuition is nature's most un-fettered embodiment, the expression of a vital force in which the senses are aroused, sharpened. And yet I never rejected reason, that little internal voice, mischievous, sometimes kindly, sometimes harmful—but always welcome. I never reject it, but it always takes a backseat.

That day, at home, with my neighbors listening to me, I felt music take possession of space, become space itself, and after it, during the pause that followed the final chord, everything res-onated around me in a way that was gay, happy. Evident.

I had already felt this force when I listened to Beethoven's Fifth Symphony, conducted by Karajan. At the time, I was completely taken up with the world of Dumas, in particular the characters in *The Count of Monte Cristo.* I would listen, and the armored phantom of the Château d'If would appear before me. I remember very well that the movements of this symphony, and those inside me, set me in motion. The raised prison surrounded by the sea, the roaring of the waves in time with the music and my swaying body, and that force that ravaged my soul, drew me into that sonorous whirlpool down toward the depths.

I think it was at that moment that I understood that the true abysses are in the sky, are of the sky, and from this, by this, true vertigo as well.

We have become increasingly interested in the psychic abilities of certain people. They have a sixth sense, an intuition that is said to give them the ability to foretell the future, to read others' thoughts, and to understand the secret links between death and life. Is it because their natures remain uncorrupted? Many animals have demonstrated the same ability: the history books are full of them.

Thus, we read that Louis XI purchased from its master the donkey Brunot, who could predict the weather.

In 1923, the frantic behavior of goldfish belonging to the Emperor of Japan—they ended up throwing themselves out of their bowl—alerted him to an impending earthquake.

Several hours before the arrival of the bombers, the dogs of Hiroshima started a frenzied howling all together.

On November 24, 1944, in Freiburg, a duck, which its owners had been watching because of its strange premonitory behavior, began quacking furiously and trying to escape by any means. Thus alerted, a good part of the population began to flee with it out of the city. Half an hour after their departure, a hail of bombs destroyed the city center and killed some thirty thousand of its inhabitants.

In Spain, a horse refused to enter a mountain tunnel, despite being struck repeatedly with the coachman's lash. Behind the cart, car owners began to honk their horns furiously. To no avail—even though some of the drivers got out of their vehicles to try to yank the obstinate animal this way and that toward the side of the road, the horse refused to budge. And no wonder: a few seconds later, the tunnel collapsed.

Six months before Les Halles, the old produce market, was moved from the center of Paris, two million rats, inexplicably alerted, began moving toward Rungis, the new address of the "belly of Paris."

For weeks, Winston Churchill's cat refused to leave the bedside of his master, who was waiting for the turnaround in his health that his doctors had predicted. Recovery was imminent. A few hours later, the cat began yowling terribly and, leaping up, tore out of the room. Churchill died the next day.

Victor Hugo, irritated by the perpetual whining of his poodle, Baron, gave the dog to his friend the Marquis de Faletans, who was about to be posted to Moscow. The diplomat adopted the dog and regularly wrote Hugo with news of the animal—until the day Baron disappeared. Despite posted announcements and the promise of a reward, the dog was not found. A few months later, thin, his paws bloodied, Baron scratched at the door of Victor Hugo's house. He had traveled more than two thousand miles to return to his master's side. . . .

And what can we say about Mohilov, the Duke of Enghien's dog, who had to be dragged away by force from his master, who was being taken away to be executed in the moat of the Château de Vincennes? As soon as he was released, the dog ran off at top speed and found his way to the cemetery where, whimpering, he lay on the duke's tomb. No doubt Mohilov would have died, had the duke not stipulated in his will that the greatest care should be taken of his faithful—his most faithful—companion.

Three

And then I met him. Up to that day, his name—which I had heard uttered at the Conservatory in Aix where I had been accepted—floated in an aura of respect and admiration. To pronounce the name "Barbizet" was to say it all: excellence, affection, admiration, and respect.

"Hélène, I'm going to take you to Marseille, where Pierre Barbizet has agreed to audition you."

I was eleven years old. The piano occupied my soul, but it had not yet cured my troubles. I attempted several times, as a sort of mental game, to put my willpower to the test, to exercise the control of my mind over my urges. Each time I lost. Despite everything, I played with passion; I loved it. I threw myself into scores, devouring them like books, although the contact with music was more physical. Sometimes in my imagination, without even approaching the instrument, I would know what touch, what pressure on the keyboard was needed to bring forth the exact right sound. I retained this power, and I used it particularly for Brahms's First Concerto and for Beethoven's Fourth, and the fugue in Opus 110.

I worked with a crazy enthusiasm and jumped ahead several grades. By age eleven I had almost finished the standard curriculum. Another eighteen months and it would be finished.

While I was at the Conservatory, I continued to work with Jacqueline Courtin. My heart never once failed to beat faster when I pushed open the garden gate, and as I approached her door, my lungs never failed to fill with pure oxygen. Her dog frolicked around me, and no matter what the season, there was always a flower ready to open just under her windows. I was her pupil and she lifted me up step by step, from a little girl to the magical status of musician. She was the one who contacted the Conservatory in Marseille, where Pierre Barbizet was the director.

"He's very nice, you'll see. I will go with you to Marseille."

I had never left Aix except for short vacations, and always in the company of my parents. The city was a completely unknown universe to me. Even though Marseille was the capital of our region, we systematically snubbed it for our summer vacations. In contrast to many residents of Aix, we preferred the mountains to the sea, and after I started the piano, we spent our summers in the Alps. I loved the dark fir trees, the rocks, the idea of altitude, the subtle change in vegetation the higher one climbed, and the air that thinned—I had the physical sensation that this was nature's ultimate disembodiment. Walking and climbing toward the heights, I observed every trace of human habitation progressively disappear. No more villages, then no more farms, and finally no more roads or power lines. Instead, as far as the eye could see, an endless land-scape in which I experienced my solitude with delight, this essential place where I could be myself, with myself, and approach the world. It is always in solitude that reality has taken shape for me, under the star of desire. It is through solitude that I learned that the only thing that is truly real is what one desires in oneself for oneself. . . .

To prepare me for the audition, Jacqueline Courtin had me work on Schumann's *Papillons*, the first movement of Beethoven's *Waldstein* Sonata, and the Fifth Barcarolle by Gabriel Fauré.

I was immediately struck by the marvelous sympathy, the empathy that existed between Pierre Barbizet and music. He stepped in two or three times to suggest a completely new way of playing, or to offer encouragement. After I finished the three pieces, we went back over a passage or two. He did not interrupt my playing, but rather guided it; his somewhat playful voice sang. In fact, it was as though his voice was ahead of the score, opening new pathways for me that were burgeoning with possibilities, with unsuspected dimensions.

As the final chords of the Fauré sounded, I turned to him, joyful, and said that I had just lived the most beautiful moment of my life.

"If you continue to play like that, there will be many more," he replied.

And then, speaking to my parents, he quickly added: "Your daughter is made for the piano. It will be her life—let her do it, encourage her, and prepare her for the entrance examination for the Paris Conservatory."

They were there in the room, happy and shining, seated next to Jacqueline Courtin, radiant with joy. We all looked at him.

Life had marked his face as if it were a masterwork, transforming his constant laughter into lines. I adored him immediately. Not for what he had just said: I knew viscerally that music and I would never be separated, that it structured me, that the fiber of my being demanded it, even if I had never thought that music could be my entire life. Alongside the music, there was still this sense of expectation, a feeling of dissatisfaction, the abyss. But the fact that Pierre Barbizet stated it in such a way filled me with incredible energy.

In the car on the way back, I listened to my parents talk with Jacqueline Courtin. Should I be put forward at the National Conservatory or not? At stake was how my time would be organized during the coming year. To prepare me for the examination, Pierre Barbizet consented to give me lessons, along with Jacqueline Courtin. But which day of the week? Which week in the month? My mother was disturbed by the sudden acceleration of events, by the turn that this extracurricular activity had taken. I could tell she was hesitant. Even if I didn't sacrifice my schoolwork for musical studies, even if I didn't spend more than two hours a day at my piano—though it occupied all my free hours—I spent no time with anyone else, and I had not made a single friend at the Conservatory.

I had always been very close to my mother; we shared the same attraction for the world of the unspoken, the unseen. We were both capable of endless gales of laughter, of making comical jokes that sent me back into hoots of merriment—and into a sense of total absurdity that I adored. But at that moment, something about me was not clear to her. Would she confuse the piano with my compulsive problems, put them in the same category, like substances that were dangerous for my stability? Finally, as the car slowed to drop Jacqueline Courtin off at her house, my father made the decision. Although he intimidated me, his Cartesian mind with its love of the rational, his quasi-mathematical mental universe, and his quest for rigor had weighed the pros and cons of the situation. He put aside his doubts; he understood without any qualms what music gave me and how happy it made me. It was settled: I would go to Marseille once a month for a year, and then we would see.

During the drive that separated Jacqueline Courtin's house from where we lived, settled into the backseat, I couldn't stop smiling. I couldn't wait to go and tell the whole story to my neighbors, to share my joy with Rock, and to sit down at the piano. I caught my father's gaze in the rearview mirror. He smiled back at me. At that moment, I understood that even though my mother was my inspiration, my father was the rock against which the waves broke; often, you are better shaped by the one with whom you disagree than by the one you feel closest to. . . .

I didn't like Marseille at all: it seemed like a skeleton blanched by the sun and covered with ants. But the pleasure of those hours with Pierre Barbizet! Very quickly, I began to hunger for his classes. He gave me an appetite for music, even devotion.

He was someone you naturally and spontaneously called "Master" because he was one. The influence he had over you, bathed in the sun of his accent and the sparkle in his eye, turned the work into something luminous. Above all, he was extraordinarily generous— he gave unreservedly, sharing everything with you in a poetry that resonated with images. He unlocked a piece using rhyme, rhythm, and color. He told stories and jokes, and everything became crystal clear. One day I read, in the booklet that accompanied his recording of Schubert, an introduction by Roland de Candé: "Pierre Barbizet did not understand the meaning of lukewarm. In the flood of his enthusiastic ideas, one always finds reflections that are original, inspiring and thought-provoking."

As I read these lines, the master's face came back to me, his twinkling gaze, his delightful knowing smile. I understood what he had taught me, even if at that age I had not realized it right away: we are music that is played by our destiny. Everyone has a key whether they know how to decipher it or not; in any case, we can be happy only when our being is in harmony with the note that expresses it. Thanks to Pierre Barbizet, thanks to the fruits of his lessons, I understood that one could spend one's life, and even waste it, looking for the philosopher's stone, until the day that one understands that it is not a question of turning matter into gold but, on the contrary, of turning gold into matter, so that it becomes exceptional moments, moments that give birth to art or kindness, the gold of sound—and simply of self.

The very great pianist Pierre Barbizet, my master, died on January 18, 1990, at the age of sixty-eight.

Each time I think of him, I remember this phrase from Isaac the Syrian: "He who has seen himself is greater than the one who has seen the angels."

"Music penetrates to the center of the soul," Plato says, "and gains possession of it in the most energetic fashion." Why did it seize me so strongly? Because music—the purest and most mysterious expression of culture—immediately thrust me into a transfigured reality of this world? Because, at its culmination, music itself disappears, leaving us facing the absolute? One day when I was eleven, I watched the movie *Excalibur,* an epic overloaded with cardboard backdrops. Wagner's *Parsifal* was used as the soundtrack. When I heard this music—although the images remained flat before my eyes, neatly ordered according to the director's wishes—unforgettable worlds overlapped in my mind, given color and shape by the music. Above all, colors dense and powerful that matched the images. For the first time, I understood something of music's mysterious nature, its power of revelation and its universality: playing Bach or a mass by Mozart is to paint icons with sound. Nights on end, this extract from Wagner haunted me, running endlessly through my head. I threw myself down at the keyboard to try to reconstruct it, until the day I found a version of it for piano. I studied it by ear and played it with abandon, in the delightful illusion that I was playing the entire score.

Did music seize hold of me because it is the extension of silence—the silence that always precedes it and that resounds at the heart of every piece? Music offers access to something outside speech, something that speech cannot express and that silence can, by silencing it. What is noise, but music without silence?

Music, with its powerful ability to seduce, contains magic—it enthralls through suggestion. It was not by accident that, in antiquity, it was considered a gift from the gods and that the ancients played it fervently; nor was it by chance that enchantment could be created by music. Sirens used their voices to try to turn Ulysses from his path, and they would have sunk the Argonauts, but the music of Orpheus, with his lyre, was more powerful than their singing and broke the spell. It was through singing that Hans Christian Andersen's Little Mermaid seduced the man she loved. And so that she would be unable to marry him, the witch demanded her voice in exchange for a beautiful pair of legs and a graceful walk—a fool's bargain! Her voice. Her singing. The only things that cast a spell on the prince.

Like a woman's perfume, music is thus powerfully suggestive and even bewitching: its perfume is the magical outpouring of its being. The female musician becomes in a certain way a siren reborn, the witch eternally burned at the stake who has regained her power: the power to charm. Except that the truly masculine man will never surrender—science, technology, and reason are there to protect him from false temptations. Thus, when a woman plays or composes, her music is no longer the sweetness that soothes. It is not Orpheus and his lyre, but the sirens and their voices, a trap that captivates in order to capture. It's all there, in these two opposing visions that have prevailed since antiquity. On the one hand, the bewitching sirens, evil creatures bent on the destruction of all those who listen to them, and on the other, the divine Orpheus, radiant, transcendent—neither bewitching nor evil, but charming and redeeming.

Franz Liszt, in the introduction to his symphonic poem *Orpheus*, described the life-giving power of the "father of song." We see him softening the hearts of stones and charming wild beasts, stilling the birds and the waterfalls, blessing all of nature with the supernatural benediction of art. Orpheus yoked lions to the plow so that they might till the fields, and harnessed panthers to pull carriages with families; he diverted wild torrents and caused these calmed streams to turn the watermills. All the creatures of the earth gathered in a circle, attentive, around the lions, nightingales ceased their arpeggios and waterfalls stopped murmuring. The one who calmed the wild waves beneath the vessel of the Argonauts, put Colchis's fearsome dragon to sleep, touched the heart of animals and plants and even Hades itself.

The inspired bard does not tame monsters with the lash but rather wins them with the lyre. Orpheus makes the inhuman human through the harmonious and melodious grace of art. Orpheus through his music converts it to humanity, in the absolute.

And me? Music converted me. It saved me.

It's odd, but I have only the vaguest memory of the entrance examination for the Conservatory. I remember the pieces I played, of course. They were the first movements of the Second and Third Sonatas by Chopin. Right from the start, I felt a natural affinity with this Polish composer: his great elegance, his extreme refinement, his preference, perhaps, for giving concerts for small groups, and his love of the night—that place of Revelations, of the Nocturne. He liked having only a few people around him, the lights lowered, and the scent of flowers filling the air. Since then, I have always had a curious, intimate—almost amorous—relationship with Chopin. When I think of him, which I cannot help doing, the image of a swan's neck comes to me, and perhaps also that of a light breeze lifting the veil of a curtain.

I love Chopin's music immensely, above all the consummate art with which he liberated the left hand for the piano. With him, the "servant of the right hand" found life, freedom, ascendancy. Chopin invented ambidextrous music—a tremendous door through which Liszt, Scriabin, Ravel, and Fauré would subsequently pass. Under Chopin, the left hand has a voice—a baritone hum of golden sounds. It has its own rhythm, it does not just accompany, it suggests, it takes liberties, it shatters the yoke of the—tiresome?— classical arpeggio to invent the arabesque, the duo, the dialogue, and the discourse. Chopin gave the left hand its own voice, requiring of it a mind-boggling virtuosity. Prestos, tarantellas, languors that are shot through with undulations and sinuosity, diadems of thirty-second notes and garlands—it takes pleasure in itself, frees itself, unfurls, in this cascade of scintillating notes, without ever losing its virile, impetuous clarity. I love Chopin for the harmony in asymmetry that he requires in the fingering of both hands and, consequently, I love him for the scope, the new plenitude that he gives the keyboard. With Chopin, the key of F, that prisoner of tight and conventional scales, is given the key to freedom. It liberates worlds for which it possesses the note: oceanic chasms, adamantine peaks, islands of giants. It suggests chaos by daring to use dissonance or voluptuousness by uniting trills and triplets. Above all, it is the companion of the night, throwing light on mysteries, and thus revealing all of the ambiguities of our souls and our destinies.

I am left-handed, and with Chopin, my dominant, guiding hand was able to give life to all of his lyrical accents, and to direct my innermost expressivity. "Do you know something of the night, Count?" wrote Villiers de L'Isle-Adam in *Isis*. At thirteen, the age at which I took the entrance examination for the National Conservatory, I knew nothing of the night, except what Chopin had allowed me to glimpse: a mystery of all being of which I was intimately aware, even if I was unable to define it. And no doubt it was via this mystery to which I surrendered that I convinced the jury at the Conservatory, because I was unanimously accepted.

Oh, my hands! I have just spoken of the part that Chopin had given to the left hand. Beautifully symmetrical, I must sing your praises, both of you, with a duty born of both friendship and recognition. My hands that loved the hands of my mother first of all—palm touching palm, warmth against tenderness—before testing the world, before imposing on it a shape, even a style. I remember your excitement as you hefted your treasure of marbles. Your pleasure at stroking the good, affectionate head of Ripp, Rock, and all the other dogs and cats encountered. Above all, I remember the thrill of touching the ivory keys of the piano, gleaming and cool in the midday darkness of Madame Tarit's salon.

My hands, which I never spared from any violence—you are

the ones who suffered the greatest number of bitten nails and ripped skin, and the ones who, always, have been the most faithful, magnificent musical tools that follow my eyes and obey them. It is said that the blind can read cards by a simple fluttering of their hands over them. I'm not blind, but I need my hands to see. They sense life and seize hold of it, and since my childhood, I have paid particular attention to them, no doubt precisely because I am left-handed.

As if it wasn't enough to be a girl. When I was small, my mother told me that, in days gone by, left-handed people were forbidden to write with their left hand, and they were forced to use their right. Every civilization has had its scapegoats, its sacrificial victims. For the Egyptians it was redheads; for others it was cats, women who were too beautiful, albinos, or blacks. And left-handed people. Why them? Because the left designates the bad side of life, the sinister part of space? No one has ever been able to give me the answer. Happily, I was not forbidden to use this hand to write. However, in the eyes of others I always read astonishment and sometimes discomfort. I will always remember my classmate at school. She turned her head away, claiming that watching me write made her dizzy, provoking in her some loss of orientation. Is that why left-handed people were bullied? To the point that even vocabulary reflects this, as when the word "gauche" implies clumsiness, and even a bit of stupidity.

"She's always been *gauche,* you see. . . ."

Today I am thrilled to have this particularity. I am a pure lefty—my left hand reigns queen, unable to be deposed. My hands are unequal: the right is larger, the left more stocky. I'm delighted not to be associated with the right hand: my entire being is left-handed. The right is the norm and order; the left is fanciful, and I'm more for fancy than for order. I'm happy being left-handed. Independent, my hands live more freely—my right hand is obliged to go beyond itself, to reinvent itself in order to meet the challenges of a repertoire that was not written for it. Together, suspended over the keyboard, my two hands sketch a multitude of possibilities in the air. Raised, then lowered, one after the other, with the agility of dancers, following incredible cadences, the fingers set bouquets of figures alight.

Oh, my hands! I don't just love you because I live from you or because I am a pianist. Our fingers are just conduits for internal energy, and when you play, your entire body—back, shoulders, arms—helps and accompanies you. I don't just love you because I feel dependent on you. On the contrary, very often I practice the piano without you. If I have always paid extremely close attention to you, it is because I have always been fascinated by the hands of others. As a child, I would force myself not to listen to the conversations taking place around me, but to guess their contents by the movements of the palms, fingers, and wrists that belonged to the various people who spoke with my parents. My mother's students, who came to the house to talk to her and confide in her, using the pretext of a class or a late homework assignment—she always attracted cheerful gatherings of adolescents. Adults, who watched their words and how they spoke, but who forgot to silence their hands. Thus, left to their own devices, they fidgeted and tensed, gripped the sleeve of a pullover (shyness?) or a handkerchief (a confessed, half-pardoned sin?) or clung to each other like two orphans.

Stiff index finger or closed fist (politician), twisting a strand of hair (ingenuous?), cupped around a face (seduction), fingers spread across the lips (incredulity), thumb sucked like a baby—all of these hands spoke volumes, like Rembrandt's hands must have spoken when they held a brush, or those of Matthew writing the gospel dictated by the angel. Oh, hands! Artists breathe in the world through their palms—I'm sure of it.

And so, a decisive page in my life had been turned. I was twelve years old and enrolled in the National Conservatory of Music in Paris. I was going to spend several days a week in Paris and several days per month in Marseille, where Pierre Barbizet continued to work with me. The question of school had to be dealt with: no junior high school would accept a part-time student. Thus, it was decided that I would enroll in the CNED, a French national educational institution that offers courses by correspondence. Education was not the only area where my age was a problem. Although there was still no minimum age at the Conservatory—the year after I was accepted, applicants had to be at least fourteen to enroll—there were many who balked at teaching those who they considered to be children.

In the summer before the entrance examination, on the advice of Pierre Barbizet, I went with my parents to the Alps, to Les Arcs specifically, where a piano workshop was held under the direction of several professors from the Conservatory. The trip was a strategic one. It was not enough to apply to the Conservatory—before being admitted, you had to go see the professors who taught there and ask if one of them would agree to accept you in class. Pierre Barbizet spoke to me about two or three of them who, in his eyes, were most closely suited to my temperament and personality. For his part, my father, ever energetic, telephoned Dominique Merlet. Their conversation was very brief. Dominique Merlet had immediately asked how old I was. "Twelve," my father replied. "In fact, she'll be thirteen in November, when she sits for the examination."

"Sorry, but I don't take students that young. They're not mature enough, emotionally speaking."

The session at Les Arcs pleased me very much—imagine a school where all they teach is your hobby. My parents relaxed. I went to classes in the morning. I had a good time, but unfortunately, Pierre Barbizet's plan was a failure: none of the professors he had mentioned to me was there.

"I'll organize a meeting with Jacques Rouvier," the master decided, when my parents explained the situation to him. "His family lives in Marseille, and he often comes to visit."

It was September, and I was back in Aix. In the streets, I met students who were getting ready to return to school. As always, the light at that time of year was magnificent, dusted with gold in the evening and clear blue in the morning, at the hour when old Provençal men, knotted like vines, and wrapped in a delicious odor of soap and eau de cologne, stepped out to buy the morning paper. I watched the boys and girls, lists in hand, crowding the aisles of the bookshops and stationery stores. Some, from my school, called out to one another. They had been in the same class the previous year, but had lost sight of one another, missed one another, guessed at which of them had been luckiest in getting into Mr. or Mrs. So-and-So's class.

For my part, I was prey to conflicting emotions. I was happy to finally escape the daily grind of school, that immutable ritual where everything is planned all the way to the end of high school. I had always felt myself to be an outsider, even odd, of another essence and another world, and here it was—an event in my life that finally bore out this profound conviction. It was the end of those recess hours, where the childish soul is given over to violence of all kinds. The end of those interminable hours to crawl through until the shrill sound of the electric bell brought deliverance. Thanks to the courses from the CNED, I was going to be the master of my time, freed from being crowded by my classmates. And finally, I would devote the lion's share of my time to the piano, my passion. My chest swelled with happiness at the thought. I could have kissed the plane trees of Aix, which seemed to wave their high branches for me alone, like palm trees. Paris? Traveling to the capital did not excite me. I was not yet at the age when one wants to leave, take flight, leave behind the family cocoon. I was twelve for another few weeks, and I was not yet in the adolescent or pre-adolescent rejection phase. In addition, Paris didn't mean anything to me; I was simply told that it was the only place where I could continue to devote myself to my passion—I had gone as far as I could with training to be found in Aix and Marseille.

For all that, between Paris and me, there was no measure of distance or image that either excited or repelled me. At night, in my bed, I had not imagined any sort of dialogue with that place, or even asked to see a book or look at photos. I felt neither anxiety nor impatience. I was simply waiting for Paris to take on a more personal name for me: that of the professor who would, if I was accepted, take me in his or her class. . . .

The summer was drawing to a close, and I was still without a professor. Whenever I entered the house, I ran to my parents to ask if they had any news. I was restless, until a phone call came from Pierre Barbizet. As promised, he had set up an appointment in Marseille with Jacques Rouvier, a professor in Paris.

In the car with my parents on the way there, I did not doubt for an instant that the audition would be a success. The final barrier that lay in the way of my passion had just fallen.

❧

According to Heraclitus, the definition of God is "day-night, winter-summer, war-peace, satiety-hunger; he undergoes alteration in the way that fire, when it is mixed with spices, is named according to the scent of each of them."

In fact, the real name in Greek of this God—so dual, so other—that Heraclitus worshipped is "Struggle." What did this strange Struggle-God symbolize? Nothing less than the original unity of all opposites, maintained in an inverse relationship to each other to the limits of antagonistic tension. But which one— day or night, war or peace—would give in? Neither, as it turns out. They are sustained in order to create a harmony among those to which they give birth: Harmony is the other name of God. But be careful! The word in Greek in no way refers to the soothing appeasement that, ever since Plato, we call harmony. The harmony of Heraclitus's God is none other than the tense meeting-place of opposing forces. This harmony is found in the marriage of opposing tensions, and only this propels the arrow from the bow. The bow? Its name in Greek evokes both life—*bios*—and the formidable weapon of Artemis, from which death shot forth.

Isn't this all just wordplay? Not completely. The double meaning of this word is where we find the very idea of the unity of opposites, thanks to which existence is given to us. We are both too old and too young to live and to die, but we live our death and die our life according to the law of God-Struggle and Harmony, whose fourth name is Time. "Time is a child that plays, it plays at moving its game pieces: oh, kingdom in which the child is prince."

If we understand this, then the movement of ebb and flow ceases to be one of thrust and drift. It is the means by which a relatively permanent level is established, which allows ships to stay afloat, to set sail, and to return to port. The movement of ebb and flow *is* the movement of struggle. Far from simplifying everything and allowing one side to gain the upper hand—day or night, war or peace—this struggle constantly enriches each side by its opposing of the other. According to Heraclitus, it is this confrontation that life forces us to take into account—the perfect equilibrium arising from this confrontation that defines what is constant. Constant? Yes, what is constant: the perfect moment of universal opposition, as long as we remain capable of conquering it.

Looking back, I understand how lucky I was and how courageous my parents were. I had just turned thirteen when I took the entrance examination for the National Conservatory of Music. No jury member put forth an objection or a veto. My parents no doubt perceived this unanimity as an encouragement: the collective voice of approval certainly quelled any final hesitations. If first Pierre Barbizet and then the highest authorities in French musical instruction had all sanctioned this path, how could they have any doubts? Yet it couldn't have, for all that, entirely calmed their fears.

Thirteen! Thirteen is still childhood. Should my parents send a child, and a girl to boot, off to a big city where neither one of them had family, or even friends, to take me in? Someone suggested a network of families that, for a fee, offered housing to students.

It was decided. I should spend two days a week in Paris, to which travel time had to be added. I "went up" to the capital by train. In 1982, France's high-speed TGV did not yet exist, and so I watched the slowly changing landscape through the windows of the Express (a name I found magnificently romantic).

Bit by bit, the North encroached on my universe. After the harsh white rocks of the Alpilles—those giant, petrified peaks against which the mistral howled, and which appeared to the east of the railroad tracks—after the beautiful carpets of blossoming almond trees, olive groves, and blue grapevines, there appeared the first green patches, meadows, marshes, and meandering waterways fenced in by the sadness of tall, nostalgic poplars. You know, landscapes are basically musical. Mountains, which I observed as a child in the hope of meeting God, are Johann Sebastian Bach. The higher you climb, the less you can see of what is below, and the more the altitude allows you to find yourself. The meandering stream is a legato. A serpent, a continuous, uninterrupted movement.

The train would stop, and then go on. The names of the stations—Valence, Lyon—punctuated my trip. During the voyage, manifestly happy to be working alone, I intently studied my CNED courses and, above all, my scores.

My scores provided me with immense solace in the hours following the train's departure. My parents carefully installed me in my compartment, my father glancing fiercely at the passengers around me, so that everyone would know that this little solitary girl was neither abandoned nor an orphan. Troublemakers beware! My mother hid her worries in a flurry of material fretting. Was I sure I had taken my toiletry kit, my pajamas? My change purse, which was attached by a leather cord to my bag in case—was it, in fact, firmly attached? "Don't forget," she said in her soft, musical voice. To take my medicine, to say good evening, to be polite. And my ticket? It had been punched, hadn't it? And what about my seasonal train pass . . .

My father, for his part, clearly pronounced, enunciating every syllable, which metro I would take, first to the Conservatory, and then to my host family. We had rehearsed the trip together during my first trip to Paris. The memory I have of that first visit remains nestled in my hand—it was of his hand: the slightly nervous grip of his fingers and, unheard-of in my father, the slight moisture on his palm, though his voice remained steady. At that instant, I understood the gift they were giving me by not attaching greater importance to their own moral comfort and keeping me locked up at home, in Aix, in a conventional educational path. But instead, they let me spread my young wings, allowing my entire being to fly toward that terra incognita that we call destiny—which for me was music.

When the train departed, I waved at them for a long time from the window. I blew them kisses; they looked like two castaways adrift on an ice floe. They acted stern and assured so as not to show any trace of their discomfort and their worries. Their last words of advice caught in their throats: "If a stranger approaches you . . ." "When class is over, don't linger, whatever you do. Go straight to your host family."

My throat tightened. I hated these departures, even if they were taking me to a place where I felt a little more at home each week and that I adored: the Conservatory.

Four

At the Conservatory, I was the youngest. Barely thirteen years old, whereas the next-youngest student was already fifteen.

Thirteen years old, with a new, magnificent freedom, as large as a kingdom, and as fruitful as an orchard. Oh, my sweet freedom that year, when I had not yet tasted its bitterness or drunk its dregs: I was in Paris to fulfill what I knew to be my deepest nature, if not my destiny. I was walking on air. My body, my entire body—shoulders, arms, back, as soon as it was connected to the piano, anchored to it by hands and fingers—I made a beautiful ship of it, a voyage, a magician's wand from which fountains of music shot forth.

A brand-new freedom that I had not even named: it had come to me at that age unsullied by any rebellion or demands. I had never felt like others, and now I would never do anything the way others did.

That year, by sharing the same studies, the same passion, and the same preoccupations as the other students, I should have been able to quell the feeling of difference. But my age didn't allow it; I stayed apart—the little one. At that age, two years is practically a generation. I understood it all the more since I had always been in a hurry to grow up. For me—and I have never changed—the years are counted like gold pieces in a treasure chest. I saw adults as the guardians of exciting secrets, gatekeepers of new and mysterious palaces, different with each birthday. I was the little one, even if I was their equal in the classroom during this first year of Conservatory, even if we shared the same expectation and—as we quickly realized—the same mutual, outright rivalry.

I was their little sister, and I immediately distanced myself from my former classmates. At night, I no longer fell into the mistral from the large school staircase that separated the various floors of the school, while they watched. I knew they were sitting at their desks in middle school, studiously copying what their teachers taught them into their notebooks. I knew that their days were like oranges—perfectly round, tightly wrapped, cut into even slices, every day identical to the previous one and the one that followed. For me in Paris, it was figs today, cherries tomorrow, as I pleased. The days were like long stretches of shoreline, indistinct of course, but their very openness instilled in me the slight, oblique fear that the unknown can produce—the experience of a new kind of vertigo, but a horizontal one.

Back in Aix, whenever I met one of my former classmates in the street or in a bookstore, a happy smile stole across my face: I had escaped them.

Every day in Paris, I widened the circle of my discoveries, at whose center was the gray building that housed the Conservatory. At the Saint-Lazare train station, I wandered the "Salle des Pas Perdus." I watched the central courtyard where taxis, like buzzing bees, gathered passengers that they carried away like pollen, this one to the Champs-Élysées, that one to Saint-Germain-des-Prés, solitary voyagers or whole families, coming to pollinate the capital from their beautiful countryside. I became intoxicated by movements in the intense buzz of colors, forms, and gesticulations around the city's department stores where, as if on the steps of the temple, vendors hawked their gadgets accompanied by incessant patter. I was amazed by one of them in particular: without stopping to breathe or losing his smile, he shoveled carrots, turnips, potatoes, and leeks into his machine—a "vegetable shredder," he called it—while thin shreds gently fell from the other side of the infernal device. The machine had an insatiable appetite.

There were vendors selling wigs, watches, scarves ("Such a beautiful souvenir of Paris!"), and above all, umbrellas. How much of the sky would be blocked out if all those umbrellas were opened up? The vendor extolled the virtues of how these little items would automatically open—once the magic button on the handle was pressed, they would unfurl with the swish of a silk dress and a burst of fireworks.

I sometimes preferred the hills to the plains, and I would go off and explore the streets around Clichy, climbing with a quick step all the way to the bridge that overlooked the railway tracks. There, leaning on the guardrail, I followed the movements of the train cars. I particularly liked the sparks from the electrical cables at the point where they met the trapeze, perched on the locomotive like an elegant top hat. I dawdled there for hours in delight.

I was the little one, and in the same way that one tolerates a younger brother or sister, the Conservatory students let me tag along with them after class to the Café de l'Europe. There, all seated in the back room, they would drink a beer. Some of them smoked: the dull *snick!* of the lighter, the faint sizzle of the burning tobacco, the heavy white smoke that was blue when exhaled. Their hands gesticulated over the sticky beer rings on the Formica tables. I envied them their age, their nonchalance. I especially adored Laurence Contini, who was five years older than I: she seemed to have been freed, at birth, from the opinions of others, from convention. One could easily guess her independence from the way she laughed, the way she tilted her head toward her shoulder, how she put her big canvas bag beside her on the banquette. You could tell that she lived her life her way and that she was accountable to no one. I would sit next to her, examining her with all my strength. Sometimes I would circle their table, my movements uncoordinated, capable as always of hugging someone in a frenzy of affection or of inserting myself uninvited into their conversations, seized by uncontrollable fits of laughter. There was also Marie-Josèphe Jude, whose beauty knocked you off your feet. She exuded something silky, an aura of deep purple velvet. She was exotic and incredibly charming. Eric Le Sage, Jean-François Dischamps, and Claire Desert answered them, and sometimes, in a single voice, they would turn to me, exasperated, and send me packing.

O joyous freedom, as juicy as a piece of fruit. It was even up to me to organize my schooling. I would open the large envelope from the CNED, and from its brown paper entrails would emerge a math professor in the silent shape of a mathematics textbook. Out would come corrections to my French homework, without the teacher's barbed comments, as well as charts for history and geography. I worked when I chose, at my own pace, always keeping mathematics for last: I reveled in its beautiful universe, its precise, remarkably sophisticated architecture.

I stuffed all these notebooks in my bag, along with volumes of sonatas—Beethoven, Brahms—an entire, unexplored musical domain, which was normal at my age. I spent a great deal of time voraciously deciphering these pieces of the piano repertoire but without any method whatsoever. I was unmethodical, undisciplined, and constantly distracted by conflicting desires. I wanted to linger in the street, avidly taking in all those unknown faces and sampling the air—the strange and specific perfume of the Métro, the odor of wet cement escaping from behind the barriers of buildings under construction, and the delicious smell of hot bread and croissants in the early morning. The desire to read all of Beethoven and Brahms, and always Chopin, but the major works, the sonatas—at once, right then and there—and the desire to rush over to the Café de l'Europe to find Laurence and the others amid the cigarette smoke and the acrid smell of beer.

Since I had passed the exemption test before entering the Conservatory, I did not have to study music theory. In addition to studying piano, I had a sight-reading class and one in music analysis.

I loved the sight-reading class, given by the marvelously cultivated Christian Ivaldi. Singers would come and perform the pieces on which we were working—nothing was either academic or laborious. The notes freed themselves from their ink and flew off in scales and intervals. . . . I had the delightfully playful notion that, at each staff, I was opening the door of a butterfly cage.

In fact, I now understand that all of my professors were exceptional and very open-minded. When you played a piece, they did not force you into a preestablished fingering. They taught you that fingering depended first on the pianist's physiognomy, on the influence of a person's body, as well as on the room, the acoustics, the instrument itself, and above all on the comfort of one's hand, with its own personal way of evolving over the duration of the score. They taught freedom, while maintaining a vigilant respect for one's personality.

I particularly respect Cortot as a musician: I have always admired his sense of invention, of musicality, and, in a way, his lack of perfection—like a loose tie around a dandy's neck. Yet I have always been astounded at the authoritarian approach of the Cortot Editions that all the conservatories use, in which fingering and pedaling are indicated in the most arbitrary fashion—in an absurd manner, in fact. Just as absurd is the way in which these editions urge students to remove difficulties from their context and work on them in isolation. If a passage contains thirds, fourths, or arpeggios that are problematic, a student should focus exclusively on them. For me, this method is the best way to create a problem where there isn't one and to invent difficulties before they even arise. When there is a real technical problem to be faced, the musical context itself provides the way to get past it—the very context that the Cortot Editions would like to isolate. When you know where you are going musically, when you know where the phrasing leads and what its colors are, then you can overcome without a hitch any technical difficulties that punctuate the musical phrase. It's like a horse stubbornly insisting on jumping over only the most difficult barrier in a steeplechase, although lacking both the momentum of the start of the race and the dynamic vision of what is to come.

I had wonderful professors, and as a result, my desire for music was never weakened. I was the little one, incomprehensibly impatient, uncompromising, still undisciplined, and forever uncontrollable. Life rubbed up against me like a cat at my feet, but I was the one who purred.

Both dolphins and the large primates transmit knowledge, new techniques, habits, and preferences among themselves. This transmission is nongenetic, purely behavioral, and can vary from one group to the next. The survival of animals in the wild depends a great deal on what has been taught to them by others. Without this transmission of information, they would die.

Frans de Waal is a brilliant ethologist and a specialist in bonobos. He posits that we can speak of culture even among animals. For him, all animals—birds, butterflies, fish—depend on this transmitted culture. In Japan in the 1950s, Kinji Imanishi, a specialist in large primates, refuted the notion that all animal behavior should be considered instinctive and all human behavior cultural. His position adhered closely to Eastern thinking, which does not oppose humans to animals, and which, consequently, never became tangled up in debates about evolution or bothered about whether humans descended from monkeys. Religion has played a major role in the different approaches of East and West. In Japan, the spirit is not the exclusive domain of human beings—it can reside in an animal, and even be passed from one animal to another.

To give an example of social learning among animals that was observed by Imanishi's students, the inhabitants of the island of Koshima fed potatoes to the island's macaques. One day a young female washed its potatoes before eating them. Slowly but surely, the others imitated her. After ten years, all of the young macaques were washing their potatoes before consuming them. Older apes never adopted this technique.

Some forty of these learned traditions that are specific to a particular group in a species have been observed in African chimpanzee populations. In the face of such proof, what ethologist would hesitate to talk about culture?

The psychologist Gordon Gallup has stated that large primates have a very evolved self-awareness. Each individual recognizes its face reflected in a mirror, and as a rule, all of them worriedly inspect the parts of their bodies in the mirror that they cannot see otherwise.

About fifty years ago, researchers began successfully teaching large primates to communicate using hand signals. Chimpanzees were taught sign language and practiced it among themselves.

At a zoo in Chicago, a three-year-old boy fell into the cage of a female gorilla and lost consciousness. The gorilla carefully picked up the toddler and, sitting on a tree trunk, watched by its own baby, the gorilla rocked the child, patting it gently on the back, just as she had seen visitors do who sat facing her enclosure.

At the San Diego Zoo, a bonobo screamed and gesticulated in the direction of youngsters who were playing in a culvert, to warn them that the floodgates had just opened. The animal witnessed this every day at the same time, and the young ones were in danger of drowning. Instead, they were saved.

It is clear that large primates and other animals have a concern for community and even possess a rudimentary moral system. Capuchin monkeys help one another to transport food, which they then share, while others will come to the rescue of one of their own caught in a tree. Orangutans will feed an older member of their species that is incapable of providing for itself.

They help, support, and console one another.

How much difference is there between men and primates, then? Barely 0.3 percent of their DNA structure.

And what is the result of this difference? Language certainly, but above all, and without any doubt, art as a human-initiated act of creation.

Then, near the end of my first year at the Conservatory, I began to fall in love.

I was not aware of it right away, no more than I was aware of the metamorphosis that was taking place in me. Until I had moved in the universe with a natural fluidity, a spectator admittedly, but one graciously received by creatures and by the world, by all flora and fauna. Between life and me there existed a sympathetic relationship and great tolerance. My wanderings around Paris had even cured me of my turbulent desires to get out of myself. If I coveted something, it was only to have the mastery of a great pianist, and the maturity and age of the other Conservatory students. When I admired someone, when that person pleased me, I was capable of throwing myself around his or her neck like a crazy puppy, overflowing with affection. I never considered the consequences of such a display. Plus, I didn't expect anything in return.

And then, without really knowing why or how, I began to stumble in the smile of others, to constantly trip over things, to bump up against existence, and to feel heavy and clumsy, weighed down by myself. "The best years of your life"—I would often hear these words then and in the years that followed. How absurd! All at once, nothing seems easy anymore. You don't know what you want, or what you are all about. Just keeping to your path becomes a trial. In fact, the best years of your life are a real purgatory.

In the same way, I heard people say, "Oh, her! It's always been easy for her. She always knew what she wanted to do, and she became a professional very young." Yes, I loved music, and my reasons for playing were visceral: I needed music to live; playing was a renaissance for me. But even though music had, up to that point, channeled my excessive psychic energy, all of a sudden it no longer seemed capable of fulfilling everything for me.

At a bookseller's stall, I happened upon a copy of Hermann Hesse's *Narcissus and Goldmund*, which became one of my favorite books. Opening the book at random, I read: "Music is based on the harmony between Heaven and Earth, on the chance meeting between the troubled and the clear." These words struck me to the core, as if they had been addressed directly to me. At that moment, the concept of "troubled" entered into my vocabulary, and I diagnosed its manifestations.

These feelings of love, for example. Doubtless, they were inevitable—classic, really. What little girl has not dreamed madly about her father, her teacher, her math tutor, or a brilliant, cheerful family friend? One of those figures who makes her lift her gaze to the heavens in order to venerate him, full of admiration for the one who possesses the keys to the world: mastery, wisdom, experience. Without knowing it, these beings—half mentor, half Pygmalion—shoot through feverish adolescent lives like meteors, stirring things up and bringing them to the boiling point.

That's how it was for me: I was stirred up. How did this transformation come about? I don't remember it chronologically, or even very exactly. I simply began to have a name and a face that stuck in my mind the way a candy wrapper sticks to one's fingertips. I was in love in my own way: compulsive, more aggressive than seductive, with cunning, friction, despair, and extraordinary resolution. And all this no doubt came at the worst possible moment—with love came a spirit of revolt, rebellion, and dissent.

Uncontrollable. Undisciplined. Unmanageable. Unbearable. The terrible time of the "Uns" was back.

Fortunately, it was time for summer vacation.

"The way Glenn Gould had of playing in the present moment gives off a lasting luminosity that brings to one's lips well-worn words like 'innocence' and 'angel,'" wrote Michel Schneider. But which angel does he mean? Nuriel, the angel of fire? Taharial, the angel of purity? Padael, the angel of mercy? Raziel, the angel of mystery, the supreme envoy of Wisdom? Or Ashriel, the angel of death, the ultimate messenger, whose beauty is mingled with dread?

Every angel proclaims. Each is a link between the divine and the human. According to the Eastern Church, human beings are located between the spirituality of the angel and the materiality of nature—their makeup contains both. But what makes humans different from angels is that they are made in the image of the Incarnation—Saint Gregory Palamas said that his spiritual part was made flesh and penetrated all of nature by its "invigorating energies." If the angel, the "second light," is the messenger of spiritual values, the role of human beings, who are reflections of the Creator, is to make these values shine forth from the substance of the world and to preserve the sources of holiness. Human beings do not reflect—they become Light, that is, creative power; this is why they are served and protected by angels.

Through playing, every musician, if he or she is inspired, brings lost Edens back to life—in the kingdom of the Holy Spirit, every angel is a musician. It is through the ear that Mary received the angel, and thus conceived. At the keyboard, a pianist is in a state of visitation. He or she vibrates with this intuition: all at once, illumination enlightens thought, guiding the body.

The angel resonates in music's wind; the same angel flies

through music with the tempest in its path; it carries the musician with it, in its wind, into the distance.

Artists are nearly always on the edge of madness. Every day they meet Jacob's powerful visitor; they struggle with the angel. Like the Archangel Gabriel, musicians at the pinnacle of their art reconnect with their mission. It is also given to them to herald the three greatest mysteries: the Incarnation, the Resurrection, and the Ascension.

A musician's body is music, and the music takes on meaning only through the body's limbs, which bring it to life: it resonates in each one of them. In the same way, at the piano, the musician is as strong as death—no more and no less, a mystical parity. When she restores the sense of time to each page of the score, the future comes to her; she does not let herself be carried off toward it. She merges all in a boundless present, and at the supreme moment, she soars, enraptured: beneath her fingers, the earth slips away into the distance.

Five

At the end of the second year at the Conservatory, students must sit for an examination, the *mention,* which assesses their levels, progress made, and areas that need to be addressed. Once this first hurdle has been passed, the student then sets his or her sights on the *prix,* which is usually awarded at the end of the third year. However, you are given three years—the third, fourth, and fifth years—to try for a *premier prix.* Thus, in the second year, students must appear before a jury with a predefined, nonnegotiable program. In my case this included, among other pieces, an étude by Chopin, another by Liszt, and a third by Scriabin.

The only thing was, this program bored me. I wasn't interested. I wanted to play the major works, the major concertos and sonatas, right away. Shorter works were no longer of any interest to me. Every week, I returned home to Aix with the same assignments written in my notebook. And the following week I would come back without having even opened the scores. Weeks and months passed. The date was approaching. I wasn't ready: I was in love.

I was in love, but once I had gotten past the torpor, the profound despair, and the moments of irrepressible euphoria, my old nature came hurtling back. Since I was compulsive in everything else, I would be compulsive in love. I decided to wage war—conquering was key. I would win the heart of my beloved like a knight in a jousting tournament, lance in hand, riding at full gallop straight at my target. Music would be my weapon, and what I lacked in maturity and femininity I would make up for by my masterful playing. And until I heard yes, I would say no—no, no, and again no, loud and clear. Headstrong and recalcitrant.

I was no longer going to be the little one, always trailing along behind the older kids. The one the others would push away, irritated, and send her back to play with her toys. I would show everyone at the Café de l'Europe—everyone at the Conservatory—that I dared to stand up to the professors, impose my views and my musical ambitions on them. They weren't going to force the little one into doing simple assignments and little pieces. The little one had big plans and big ideas. I would make it a point of honor to take no interest in that which had been imposed by the system. And since I couldn't skip calendar years, couldn't grow up any faster, then I would skip classes, just as I had done at the Conservatory in Aix.

Thus, at that age of confused hopes, with the zeal of a schoolgirl determined to be the first one to the top of the tree, I threw myself into the conquest of love. The first difficulty I encountered was not inconsequential. I would have to make myself noticed by the loved one, so that he would focus his celestial gaze on me, and then, convinced of my worth, he would succumb and throw himself at my knees—no, what am I saying!—at my feet. . . .

So, what does a child do when she wants to draw attention to herself? She resists, stamps her feet, makes her presence felt—becomes a pest. My best form of resistance has always been to brandish my point of view. Fueled by ridiculous dreams and weird follies, unaware that my behavior was essentially being controlled by the fact that I was becoming a woman, by the mystery of my very being, I became obstinate in my opposition, particularly my opposition to the mandatory program. I would arrive in class without ever being prepared. Of course, the only thing I succeeded in doing—which was logical—was to exasperate everyone around me. I was well and truly a little monster.

One day, at the end of his rope, my piano teacher said to me, "If I can't instill some sense of discipline in you, we're going to have to think about moving you into another class. I'm going to send you to Dominique Merlet."

This was supposed to terrify me. Can you terrify an artist? I shrugged my shoulders. Was such a pitiful, unimaginative threat going to keep me in the meager pastures of a limited musical education, leading solely to the second-year exam? I wanted to roam the vast, wild mountain ranges of the piano repertoire and, within that, to pick out only the pieces that pleased me.

"Don't come back to class unless you can play me the Chopin étude."

Chopin? Another étude by Chopin? Since they refused to see, I would show them all. I would prove it to them.

That evening I was back in Aix, having temporarily withdrawn from the class. On the music stand of my piano, I had indeed placed a piece by Frédéric Chopin, my composer. But it was not a simple étude, no, but rather the Second Concerto. I was raring to go, fiercely intent on proving I was right. Unfortunately, nothing could help me smoothly read it or make the difficult transition from reading to playing.

A week went by, with each day bringing its share of problems. Especially since I had no intention whatsoever of backing down or making amends. I wanted to play this great work. I strengthened my determination by picturing scenes from my future triumph—my imagination illuminating them like chandeliers in a theater. All at once, with a wave of my wand, all of the professors from the Conservatory, and all of the students with them—and Him, above all Him—all of them assembled in the auditorium of the Paris Conservatory, were listening to me, enraptured. And I, fearless, nonchalantly casual, I played Chopin's Second Concerto with brilliant mastery. In an instant, I supplanted all the great pianists who had come before me.

I had them under my sway, had them in my power. I played and made light work of the difficulties. I excelled. They could only applaud and admit defeat. . . . Oh, but my triumph would be a modest one! As soon as the last chord sounded, without taking a bow, I would head for the exit. Would my gray eyes then meet His—at last admiring, dazzled, amorous?

At this moment in my imaginary film, I varied the endings. Sometimes, when the notes would start to swim on their staffs, afloat on tears of fatigue, I opted for direct confrontation—my gaze lashing His. Tough? Triumphant? Docile? Beseeching? Other times, I preferred ostentatious disdain. So He treated me like a child, like a baby? Now it was my turn to ignore Him!

"Did you know that the Aix Conservatory has created an orchestra of the professors and some of the upper-level students?"

My mother was singing to herself in the kitchen. I was circling around her like a lioness in a cage, impatient to prove my worth. She had lifted her face in my direction, stopped her hands in midair on that spring evening to smile at me, and then had gone back to preparing her recipe. I threw my arms around her neck, as I always did, to smother her with kisses. Without knowing it, she had found the solution to my puzzle.

I was fourteen years old, with no inhibitions to stand in my way, and full of daring. The next day I was back at the Aix Conservatory, where I had been a student for four years.

"I want to work with you. And I would like it to be the Second Concerto by Chopin."

There was no mockery, no irony, no sending me back to work on a nocturne or an étude on the straight path to the *mention*. On the contrary, they welcomed me happily. They had known me before Paris. They knew the affectionate esteem that Jacqueline Courtin held me in, and about the classes with Pierre Barbizet. And, in short, they wouldn't say no to my coming back home to play this piece. . . .

"Do you know that the orchestra's goal is to give a concert at year's end? Will you be with us?"

A concert? My first public concert? Why did I have to be so in love, and thus blinded by my secret, personal plot? I felt no enthusiasm and no excitement, and just as little fear, doubt, or nervousness at the idea. I just felt thrilled to have found the way: finally, I was going to learn a great work, rehearse it at home alone, and practice according to my intuition. The number of variations became infinite, the shimmering colors, the tempos running free "where reason and magic become one."

I threw myself headlong into the work. My reason for playing was visceral, and so I played well, magically in tune with the world. I wanted to conquer and to find myself. I was so acutely conscious of this happiness, of my need for music in order to live, and of the renaissance with which this piece filled me, that I became physically aware of how precious the process of working was. All at once, psychologically, I relented and began to study, in addition, the études by Chopin, Liszt, and Scriabin.

I wasn't just delighted; I was exalted. Filled with an inner quivering, aware that I was forging my real self with an entirely new rigor—rigor and strength. I went about my conquest in my own way, impulsively and passionately, with the tempo set at *allegro affettuoso*—in other words, fast, expansive, with feeling, considered but always instinctive—without any sense of moderation. I did only what I wanted to do, and even today, when what I want is not possible, I see to it that it becomes possible. The definition of passion is throwing oneself headlong into what one does, body and soul, with neither hesitation nor inhibition—that was how I did things and how I continue to do them. You make a few mistakes with this method, but so what? They are the sorts of errors that make life interesting and they hurt only you. All in all, it's a fairly harmless approach.

And then came the day of the concert. I had the feeling that I was finally living, living in broad daylight, publicly, the thing I had been silently waiting for all my life. First there was the piano, friendly, glimmering in the half-light of the stage like a heartfelt smile. Then came the first measures from the orchestra, which poured their clarity over me in a flowing dialogue, laying their volatile chords across my hands. At the same time, I was released to be completely myself, unmoored, borne aloft by the brand-new and delightfully breathtaking feeling of absolute freedom.

Music had freed me.

It was my fourteenth year.

I was no longer little.

Among the Scandinavians, in the Great North, a wolf was brought up by the gods. His name was Fenrir, and he was fearless, unpredictable, and intractable. He broke every chain that was placed around his feet, and only the god Tyr dared to feed him. One day, in an attempt to tame the creature, Tyr created a special chain called Gleipnir, which was both unbreakable and elastic. So that he might be persuaded to have it slipped around his neck, the gods asked Fenrir, as a favor, to break this chain. Fenrir accepted, but since he suspected something, he asked that one of the gods place his hand in Fenrir's mouth as a guarantee. This, then, was how Gleipnir, the magic chain, fettered Fenrir forever, and how the god Tyr lost his hand. Ever since then, Scandinavians have awaited the "time of the wolves," which will mark the end of the cycle of the world—the time when the ever-growing Fenrir will see his chain fall away and he will dissolve the universe.

This cycle of the world is the cycle of the seasons. When Odin and his wolves die, the world will be purified and experience a new morning, a tender green spring—because springtime is green, isn't it? And blue as well, at dawn. That is, as long as Geri and Freki, the wolves of Odin, don't succeed in devouring the sun and moon, at the end of the infinite pursuit in which they are engaged.

For this power, alchemists invoke the wolf as alchemical mercury, the universal solvent, *materia prima*, Mercury of the Wise— also known as antimony. For this power, the ancient name of winter in southern Germany is *Wolfsmond*, the month of the wolf. When Fenrir and the gods have finished doing battle, water will cover the earth, allowing a new world to emerge, and it is through his destructiveness that the wolf will make it possible to pass from one state to another. In the Romanesque cloister at Monastier, and on the church at Rozier-Côtes-d'Aurec, in southern France, depictions of a wolf with a broad tail and a devil with a wolf's head recall these Celtic beliefs.

Like us, the wolf has a double nature, a double status. Thus, Apollo—Lukeios, the god "born of the wolf"—is also the god of light. Both Cyrus the Great, founder of the Persian Empire, and Genghis Khan were nurtured by a she-wolf, not to mention Romulus and Remus, of course. The she-wolf, symbol of fecundity, suckled Ailbe, one of the first Irish saints, as well.

The wolf has the reputation of being able to see in the dark— the ring of Saint Loup cures blindness, and the blind Saint Hervé was guided by a wolf, which saved him from death.

Francis, the good saint from Assisi, converted the wolf that had terrorized the town of Gubbio, calling the creature "Brother Wolf."

And on a wild wolf was tamed by the beauty and music of Saint Austreberthe, who brought the creature to heel.

Providential chance and incredible signs of destiny.

The concert given by the Aix Conservatory was recorded for the archives, and I was kindly given a copy. I thus possessed the entire Second Concerto by Chopin, performed by me, and since it was impossible to replay this work in its entirety, the tape also contained the famous compulsory études, which I had played following the enthusiastic "encore" from the audience.

Now I was going to impress them, all of them.

Off to Paris! And then—consternation.

"Well, look who's back! Mademoiselle Grimaud!"

Everywhere the same chilly reception—or, at best, the same astonishment—at seeing me walk back through the Conservatory door, admittedly after a month away. The whole school administration had the same idea: to punish my absence.

"Do you think we're some kind of hotel? A self-service restaurant?" Oh, so I had taken the statement "Don't come back to class until you can play the required program" literally? Well, too bad for me. At my age, and being just a student, I was in no position to get so worked up or to be too sensitive.

I had dreamed about an audience, and instead I found a tribunal. I had to clear my name, excuse my little vanishing act, prove that I had been working, prove that I knew those études like the back of my hand, and quickly—not study piano anymore in this school? Then where? This was madness!

I wouldn't let them do it. I had the proof of my efforts and my work in my bag. Just a minute! Please, just give me a minute! You have to listen to this recording. . . . Deftly pulled from my bag, the cassette of the concert stood at the tips of my fingers. I waved it. My proud eyes, sure they were in the right, punctuated my gesture, my regrets, my entreaties. In front of me, there was nothing except a skeptical silence, worn out by my restlessness—I am still restless, by the way; it's chronic with me, even when I was fourteen, and when I'm in love.

Silence isn't the same thing as a refusal, is it? Wordlessly, so as not to break the fragile equilibrium of the moment held in the faces of my judges, and attentive to the slightest twitch, frown, or clenched jaw that would order me to stop, I slid the famous cassette of the concert in Aix onto the desk of Jacques Rouvier, my piano teacher. My professor did not push it back. He even, thank God, agreed to listen to it. That recorded concert would save me. My reputation of being an immature child would, at the same moment, be demolished. In addition, since the applause had not been removed from the tape, I would be able, without explanation, to affirm my triumph. . . .

"See you tomorrow in class," Rouvier said, almost curtly.

I turned on my heel and left the room, and then went back to the ranks as if nothing had happened. And really, what had happened? Nothing that could not be reduced to an administrative footnote, a little bump in the road. (A student in my class simply asked, "Were you ill?") I was back, still in love, and still aiming for the same goal: to be loved. But the episode of Chopin's Second Concerto and the concert in Aix had reached a deep place that was elsewhere, beyond love and beyond school. With my arrogant insistence on playing and learning by myself, I had managed to go right to the heart of my life, and of emotion.

What a stroke of luck! Yoshiharu Kawaguchi, at the time the principal producer for the record company Denon, was passing through Paris. He wanted to discuss the program of an upcoming CD that Rouvier was to record with Jean-Jacques Kantorow, and the meeting was scheduled for around this time.

When they met, my piano teacher pulled out my cassette.

"Here, listen to this recording and tell me what you think."

"Who is it? I want to record them," Kawaguchi said, once he had listened to the cassette.

"Hélène Grimaud, one of my students," Rouvier replied. "But she has to earn her *premier prix* before recording anything whatsoever. That's about a year and half from now, at the earliest."

Three weeks later, Kawaguchi was again in Paris. I was in piano class playing when he arrived. He sat quietly at the back of the room and listened to me.

When I had finished, he stood up. He cleared his throat and said, very simply: "For your first recording, I'm very interested in what you are playing."

It was Liszt. I had other ideas, and a very precise idea at that. I turned abruptly on the piano stool to face my visitor. In a firm voice, my gaze unflinching, I said: "I would prefer Rachmaninoff."

Scientists agree that the wolf was the first animal to be domesticated by humans. How did this happen? In prehistoric times, human beings became hunters to feed themselves, hunting in groups. They shared among themselves the meat from the prey they had captured and killed. Social relations were thus invented, as well as the sedentary lifestyle. The first villages and the first lake dwellings appeared; the first animals were domesticated. In the late Paleolithic era (12,000 B.C. in subarctic regions and about 8000 B.C. in northern Europe) wolves were friendly with humans, long before any other animal would be domesticated by sedentary farming communities. That wolf, *Canis lupus*, appeared some 2 million years ago. It was smaller than the wolf we know today, and had descended from its distant ancestor, of the family Miacoidea, which lived between 54 and 38 million years ago in North America. This animal was originally a tree-dweller that gradually adapted to terra firma, becoming *Canis lupus*.

From time immemorial, humans and wolves lived side by side, and in a similar fashion. Both species hunted the same prey across a shared territory. Simultaneously, if not together, they tracked the seasonal migrations of herbivores. No doubt, albeit only occasionally, they hunted each other when one group felt threatened by the other. The discovery of large deposits of wolf bones in the Ukraine, dated to about 20,000 years ago, is proof that humans eliminated sizable numbers of wolves, probably to use their hides to cover themselves.

In addition, humans probably observed the wolves' more experienced hunting techniques, and took up positions along the path of the prey they were pursuing. For their part, wolves drew near to human encampments in order to devour the scraps that the two-legged animals had left behind. Finally, out of curiosity or amusement, men gathered up the pups of adult wolves that had been killed during a hunt. They probably gave these pups to the women of the group, who nourished them—either by breast-feeding them or by giving them premasticated pieces of food.

At present, there is no proof for this theory, but it seems perfectly plausible to the majority of the scientific community. Women breast-feeding animals whenever hunters return to the village with the young of animals that have been killed is a practice that can still be seen in a number of societies. In parts of Siberia, the Amazon, Oceania, Tasmania, Africa, and occasionally Europe, women breast-fed wild animals, which they then kept close to them.

According to the ethnologist Jean-Pierre Digard, women have nursed puppies, piglets, peccaries, monkeys, fawns, and lambs. The animals became companions for children and served as de facto garbage collectors, and as small heat generators to combat cold nights. In France in the nineteenth century, women suckled puppies for relief if their breasts had produced too much milk or, conversely, to start the milk flowing. In addition, animals also were used in certain religious practices, like the bears tamed by the Ainu on the island of Hokkaido in Japan.

According to the Ainu, the bear is a member of the divine pantheon, and his spirit is the messenger of the gods. When the bear is killed, his spirit returns to the upper worlds, from where it protects those who have freed it. For this reason, hunters take very young cubs from their mothers and give them to the women in the village to nurse. The bear cubs grow up with the children in the family. Then, when the bear is three years old, it is led through the village in a ceremonial procession during an annual festival that takes place in the autumn. After this, the villagers surround the bear and wound it with arrows until the animal is in an uncontrollable fury. Then it is killed by being crushed between two logs. During the killing, the women perform ritual dances while the men and children weep copious tears. Finally, the animal's flesh and entrails are eaten in a feast in which the entire village takes part. This same ceremony is practiced in Siberia—the bear is fed on gruel before being sacrificed, and the women sing a funeral chant as the animal is being put to death.

But to return to our original pair: humans and wolves. The wolf pup must be socialized, and socialized relentlessly, from when it is only a few weeks old. The social bonds that the animal will maintain later in life are formed in earliest infancy. To make the deepest imprint, the best and most efficient means of socialization involve physical contact—caresses, games, looks, and keeping the pup close by—as well as bringing food even before the pup is weaned. The human imprint expands the animal's behavior, with the decisive and radical result that the animal becomes habituated to human beings. It is in this way that the ancient hunting companionship between humans and wolves resulted in the latter being tamed by the former.

A tamed wolf became a very efficient hunting companion, because it brought game back to its master. Wolves also became of vital importance during the Paleolithic era, when climate change caused an upheaval in the lowland distribution of herbivore mammals, which began to migrate much more rapidly. To hunt them, humans needed help, and had to fashion more efficient and more easily manageable weapons. They used wolves to track and, above all, to pursue game.

At the same time, the tamed wolf, with which the hunters shared their prey, became dependent on humans for food. Selectively bred, the animal lost qualities inherent to the wild species and gradually evolved toward the dog—it became smaller, its shape changed, and its muzzle shortened. This is what is called neoteny, i.e., the retention of juvenile characteristics in the adults of a species.

❧

The uproar didn't last long. I wasn't expelled from the Conservatory, and I played the Chopin études, as agreed and required for the *mention*, which I obtained without any trouble. However, I had been quite afraid. I'm not really sure what frightened me more: not seeing Him anymore or no longer learning music. Whichever it was, both hypotheses had seemed completely intolerable to me. I thus resolved to calm my rebelliousness, and I ordered Miss Hyde to give way to Dr. Jekyll. Things slowly settled back into place at the end of the second year. I had the same two very precise ideas in mind, but henceforth I favored their more sensible versions. I still had my sights set on conquest—winning both the *premier prix* and the heart of my beloved. I rapidly became aware that my passion for the piano and my skills could only help me to achieve the second objective. I thus began to work seriously and passionately, helped along my path by exceptional professors who were remarkable teachers. I spent a great deal less time wandering the streets.

Work was not the only reason that I left off the wanderings of my first months in Paris. I still liked to roam just as much, and I still dreamed of those capital cities that the surrounding streets were named after, as the trains' roar carried me off toward them. Rome, Amsterdam, London—all of those elsewheres whose names I recited under my breath, and which seized my heart with a premonitory nostalgia. I continued to go for walks and visually devoured the faces I met, trying to retain their shape, to learn them by heart so that, in the evening, alone in my room, I could make them play out the myriad stories that I made up about them. A certain woman—whose lithe, floating gait revealed the mystery of her being—was given the lead role in my improvised troupe of actors. Sometimes ugly faces moved me deeply, and old ones as well—perhaps they were even my favorites, those lined faces that bore the entire geography of a life. The balance between the weight of years and the fragility of those lives struck me to the heart. Some gave the impression of birds waiting for the great winter migrations, their wings folded with arthritis, heads sunk into their shoulders. In my dreams, I placed their silhouettes on the overhead power lines at the Saint-Lazare train station, enormous staffs on which they became the notes. I composed symphonies from them. There was a bass clef of beings with soft,

smiling eyes and talkative lips, and a treble clef of children—
those who let their dogs find paths in the street other than the order of the sidewalk and the dullness of the asphalt.

In fact, I never really tired of these promenades, but I was now
fifteen years old, and my way of staring at strangers—even though
I didn't really mean anything by it—began to trigger responses. I
was no doubt partly responsible. My gaze is often disturbing. My
photo on the cover of my solo Brahms CD led someone to remark
that I was "a visionary, clearly under the influence of cocaine."

Men began to smile at me, smiles that were terrifying because
they were neither kind nor gentle—smiles that were sticky like
dirty candy. There are a thousand variations of the lecherous gaze.
Some are quietly ironic, and some are more timid—but with
something obscene underneath. I met gazes lit up with a volup-
tuous twinkle. Looks of infinite melancholy—those who have
sworn off forbidden fruit and who dream of tasting it, poisoned
each day by the strychnine of their desire. For me, as for every girl
in the world, this inspection of which I was the object—and the
gleam in those eyes, directed toward me—had something chilling
about it, because it gave off a primal, barbarian essence, a pure
and nuclear violence, a glimpse of huge, black, ferocious forces.

And yet, looking back, I think that this way was much simpler
than the attitude that some men have toward me now. In the
streets of my fifteen-year-old self, there were patent invitations
from some men, despite the fact that my legs were as thin as
poppy stalks, despite the lack of any concern about my appearance, and despite my baggy sweaters that hung down to my knees,
my sleeves nibbling at my hands. These invitations were born of

the misunderstanding created by my gaze directly meeting theirs, and my wandering stride. Today it's worse. Men don't see me; they see what they think I am. They project onto me a deformed image of themselves, their desires, and their inhibitions. And I am less and less tolerant, in these face-to-face meetings, these chance encounters that are obligatory in my profession, of being the recipient of a fantasy that is not me. I flee from it, and I have the utmost contempt for the person in whom I sense it.

It's just that men (and how few real men there are among men!) see me in a very curious manner. The combination of my qualities seems incompatible to them—a physique that could be my fortune (just sit there and look pretty) and a demanding, elitist profession; a success due not to this physique but to hard, grinding work (what a waste!), and an avowed, active passion for a pack of wolves. They juggle these various elements, trying to put them together like pieces of a puzzle that has to be assembled, and they fail. How to make the pieces fit, fit them properly together? Let's see, she's a pianist (hence someone pure), a classical musician (therefore with intellect), with an international career (thus financially independent and free to do as she likes). Until then, everything is still okay. But throw in "lives with wolves" (therefore filled with fantasies of sexual power) and my looks, and all sorts of fantasies come out.

I sometimes see that lecherous gaze in women, and it's not any easier. My meetings with certain women are not necessarily simpler—immediately I become a rival at best, and at worst an enemy. For someone for whom appearances never mattered, I am the victim of my own—that's the worst! As someone who dreams of simply making friends, instead I discover the laser beam of a gaze that weighs me, sizes me up, and rejects me, frightened. I can very easily begin to feel as though I had the plague, that I was a demon, someone in search of people's souls like the witches they burned at the stake.

Before those walks in the Parisian streets, whenever the world brushed against me, rubbed itself on me, it was through colors, smells, skies, and sheer giddiness. I wanted to escape my body and melt into all that happiness. In Paris, the world was surrounded by barbed wire. It's not that I rejected this power to disturb people, or systematically refused every narcissistic temptation. It was just that no sooner had I discovered it than I realized that I did not control it. Of course I wanted to light some fires, but at the time and place of my choosing, certainly not just because of my looks or the effect of my smile or because of my pretty eyes. To set fire to someone's passion, yes, but because of my musical vision, my ideas about the world, or my connection with the piano—a relationship that made me regret that, in all the musical mythologies and mythical bestiaries, there was no trace of a centaur that was half man, half piano, or a mermaid with a body of strings and chords.

To extinguish the gaze of men on the prowl, I learned to give my walk an almost athletic determination. Nothing is worse than nonchalance, that particular wandering stride, to trigger ambiguities and misunderstandings. Yet despite everything, in spite of my good sense, I was unable to avoid every come-on—a winking eye, the enticing jerk of a head. So I went out much less often. Besides, the city, which I didn't really like, although I adored wandering about in it, attracted me less and less. I was focused on my new projects. I threw myself into them compulsively. I dreamed of making that record; I wanted it, and I wanted it now. I was carried away by how easily my choice of composer had been accepted. Yes, I had wanted to play a great work, and I was going to record one, and one I had selected—Rachmaninoff, Opus 39.

Of course, I had to meet the conditions: a *premier prix*, and fast. I got it, the summer I was fifteen.

That summer, I dreamed for the last time the dream of the stairway, of falling in the howling mistral down into the abyss of my old school in Aix. The day after I dreamed it, I fell upon a strange story—divinatory or premonitory—that seemed to speak directly to me.

In order to look out over the loveliest landscape in the world, you have to climb to the top of the Tower of Victory in Chittaurgarh, India. Only those who do not believe in the legend dare to climb all the way up to the circular terrace at the top of the structure, taking the winding stairway that leads there. This is because on the stairway there has lived, since the beginning of time, the A Bao A Qu, an inert being that awakes when it perceives human values.

The A Bao A Qu lives on the bottom step of the winding stairway. The presence of a human being animates it: the vibrations given off by the approaching person renews its life and the light within it. Its body shivers, and its skin, nearly translucent, begins to warm and become opaque. As soon as someone starts up the stairs, the A Bao A Qu sticks close to the visitor's heels, sliding behind him or her, keeping to the worn edge of the steps, where generations of pilgrims have passed. At each level the color of the creature's skin becomes more intense, its shape nears perfection, and its interior light shines brighter. But the A Bao A Qu can reach the top of the tower and the circular terrace only if the climber is a spiritually superior being; if so, the creature will find fulfillment and achieve its perfect shape.

If the climber has, for a single day, a single minute, a single second, chosen the path of dishonor, the A Bao A Qu becomes paralyzed halfway up. It stands frozen on a step, its body incomplete, its glow dimming, and its color draining away. Before it fades completely, however, the A Bao A Qu begins to weep. Its moan, barely audible, is reminiscent of the rustling of silk, the song of wind in the bamboo trees, or the caress of the trade winds in the middle of the Atlantic Ocean. It is like the sound of something rending, breaking, *calando* in musical terms, meaning a yielding, a slowing in the tempo and the intensity of the note. One could also call it *ritenuto* or *meno mosso.*

Some say that the A Bao A Qu can see with its whole body, and that at sunset its skin has the velvet feel and sun-touched blush of a peach.

But if the man or woman who climbs in search of the loveliest landscape in the world is pure, then the A Bao A Qu attains its definitive shape, it glows with a blue light, blue like Chopin's favorite hour. At last it can breathe; it becomes breath and vision. Unfortunately, its ascension to its perfect form and state is a brief one—the visitor, his or her senses filled with the beauty of the world, must sooner or later begin the descent. The A Bao A Qu, which cannot stay on the terrace by itself, follows its guide. It rolls and tumbles down to where it started. Upon return, despite the splendors it has glimpsed, despite its former fullness, it mourns, in its torpor, the beauty it has contemplated, the freedom, the enlightenment.

The story told by Scheherazade goes on to say that, over the centuries, the A Bao A Qu has reached the top of the steps—and hence perfection—but a single time.

❧

I loved the music of Rachmaninoff immediately, and among his concertos, I feel closest to the Second. In contrast to other pieces—such as the Third Concerto, whose opening phrase reveals everything—the Second Concerto does not suffer from any redundancy. Rachmaninoff was an extremely elegant, highly aristocratic composer. I like that he always had the courage of his convictions; he went against the language of his period. At a time when revolution was everywhere in the air, when movements were being born that would enlist Ravel and Bartók (both of whom were his contemporaries), Rachmaninoff remained immutably attached to the tonal system. He was faithful to Russian Romanticism and to those musical forms on which Tchaikovsky had so gloriously left his mark. Better than anyone else, he bequeathed to the piano all its possibility to express an unbearable beauty, the path between all that is possible and the sorrow at having to renounce this glimpsed paradise—accessible through music since it has no need of angels: it is the message. Rachmaninoff is both the last Romantic composer of the twentieth century and the inspiration for the great Russian and American concertos that would be written afterward. Beyond nostalgia, with him there remains the lyrical, inextinguishable power of song. Beyond the torture that racks the Russian soul, there remains a purity of heart and of vision. From the very first notes of a piece by Rachmaninoff, we are caught in the confidence and the decency of this nervous soul, which music had saved from confusion. There is something of an apotheosis in this approach that both attracted and delighted me. And what a life! To be born in Oneg in 1873, in the far reaches of the province of Novgorod, and to die in 1943 in Beverly Hills! To have lived through two conflagrations: the Russian Revolution that drove him from his native land and the Second World War, which ushered in the era of every sort of apocalypse.

As a child, I came upon a portrait of the composer. I was fascinated by the fixed, serious gaze that emanated from that long, tormented face, the thick mouth, and the huge hands that seemed capable of gathering up all the octaves and binding them into a bouquet of flowering notes. Sergei Rachmaninoff looked at me; I truly felt as though he was watching me—me—at the precise moment the portrait was made, his back to his native country, a world away from his Slavic countryside, from onion domes and crisp crocus bulbs. I spent hours staring at those eyes, those parabolic ears attuned to the breath of the world, and those hands. Those eyes that had seen the notes of the Second Concerto before even conceiving it, those ears that had heard them, and the hands that had first written and then played them.

Was it for this reason that I always felt so tenderly toward the Second Concerto? For a long time, its story—the story of a rebirth—left me pensive. Sergei Rachmaninoff was twenty-seven when he wrote it. Encouraged by Tchaikovsky, he had already had a great success with his opera *Aleko*, which he had composed in 1892, at age nineteen. Five years later, he presented his impatient admirers with his Third Symphony. The response from both critics and the public was icy—it was a resounding failure. Rachmaninoff, whose health was fragile and whose mental stability was precarious, plunged into a terrible depression; he thought that his creativity had fled. Days and nights at the piano lit no spark whatsoever. He slid, slowly, inexorably, aware of his fall and at the same time of his inability to prevent it. Happily, 1897 was the era of Freud and the hope offered by psychoanalysis. Rachmaninoff began treatment.

His time in the wilderness lasted three years. And then, miraculously, at the end of the analysis and treatment he had undergone, he wrote the Second Concerto. It was a new start, an irrepressible surge toward something else. At the same time, this musical phrasing allowed him to escape his instability and his depression, even though now and then he would suffer a relapse. Listen closely: often, right from the first movement, you can hear the bell toll; it marks Rachmaninoff's mourning of what he did not like in himself, even though he stopped worrying about his image and about what others thought. The first movements are those of a work that is unquestionably threaded with conflict.

These contortions of the soul enchanted me. In my life, as in the work, I experienced great tensions and moments of intense reconciliation with myself. Memories of heartbreak, moments of contentment, and the acceptance of the way of the world.

I wanted to study this piece, and I wanted to play it. Through it, I felt that love and music were capable of everything; everything except "nonbeing."

Playing Rachmaninoff's Second Concerto was "being," it was like writing a letter of confession, expressing my innermost self in an immaterial tonality.

It was a way of offering myself to the one who did not see me.

❧

Everything seemed strange and new. Amsterdam first of all, where the compact disc was going to be recorded. A city of dolls' houses, more like an illustration from a child's picture book than a postcard. It was my first professional trip abroad, and I was treated like a professional, with an immense amount of deference and, at the same time, a respect that was impersonal and completely mechanical. In other words, it was the exact opposite of what I had experienced at the Conservatory, where, probably more than anywhere else, the idea of "education," the notion of apprenticeship, and the verticality of the relation between master and pupil are instilled, but always in a strongly supportive relationship. The teaching is tailor-made, and the individuality of each student is respected.

I was, simultaneously, completely unaware of the importance and the rarity of what had happened to me, and completely impressed. The tiny hall was resplendent, like a treasure box that held a jewel. And what a jewel! A magnificent piano, one of the most beautiful I had ever played. From the moment I sat down at the keyboard, I forgot about the reason I was there—the CD—and the probable consequences of this recording. I was entirely caught up by the physical pleasure of playing, with the certainty that everything was within my reach, that it was within my power to push the limits of what was possible. I remembered the emotion that had shot through me like lightning when I had heard the Second Concerto of Rachmaninoff for the first time. From the first measures, the notes unfurl, relentlessly stirring one's soul. I had been dumbstruck by the scope, the incredible power with which this piece embodied the world of Dostoyevsky—a world into which I plunged each evening, in the rooms my parents rented for me with various host families; a world that, page after page, magically erased the houses, streets, suburbs, the miseries, and the lies. . . . I was immediately haunted by one obsession: one day I would play this concerto. One day I would penetrate its depths.

Before recording the CD, I felt for the first time the symptoms that ever since I have always felt the day before giving a concert. The morning of the rendezvous, in the studio in Amsterdam, I suffered what I would call the adrenaline phenomenon. My heart began beating faster, the blood left my extremities. My breathing was broken up by hyperventilation. I was extremely focused, and at the same time my head was completely empty, my legs were like jelly, and my stomach was churning wildly. None of these sensations is pleasant, but one has to learn to accept them, to live with them, and, if you can't get over them, to control them.

That day, as I do now before going onstage, I began to do breathing exercises. I empty my lungs. I breathe deeply from the diaphragm, I learn to control the flow of my breathing. The blood begins to flow differently; by doing this exercise, I am able to center myself and put my brain into an alpha phase. At the same time, I create mental projections; I concentrate on imagining three things. I focus on the first, then the second, and then all three together, like the three cherries on a slot machine. This technique pulls me into a rhythm that allows me to reach an inspirational level. The idea is to perfectly control one's breathing while focusing attention on the images that arise. Focusing the brain in this way is like going into a trance, or reaching an ideal rhythm, as with Buddhist mantras. The goal is that, as the exercise progresses, the brain ceases to form distinct thoughts.

There's another exercise that I particularly like: I imagine a place that I like, or that I would like to visit, such as the terrace of a tower from which you can look out over the loveliest landscape in the world. You see a stairway: at the bottom of this stairway is a room with a door. You open the door, go into the room, and there you discover something or someone. Most often, what you find is someone dear to you or someone who is gone—which is, in fact, our own internal voice.

What I learned from my first recording, so rich in teachings, was that one has to pay attention to the body—but I mean this in a spiritual sense. We all suffer from repetitive movements. We all learn habits as we get older, when what we should be doing is unlearning them. We need to learn how to better move our arms, our head, our torso, and our legs. Most people don't know about their muscles; they're not aware of them. They don't know anything about themselves. Who knows anything about neuronal currents, the origin of our nerve impulses, our chance to evolve? The body conditions reasoning. Unlearning the body's daily habits means an opportunity to have a different relationship to one's thoughts.

The day of the recording was a normal day for me. I experienced those first hours as I did every other concert or competition recital. I was quite simply happy to be with a magnificent piano, and to have the chance to be able to play repeatedly, several times in succession, passages I wasn't satisfied with. For the first time, I did not feel the pressure of time—the tempo of classes timed to the minute, the tempo of the score determined by the orchestra. There was no closing time, no moment that we absolutely had to be out of the studio. A recording—even though the audience's reaction, the immediate emotion, is sacrificed—offers the luxury of discarding early choices that are no longer suitable, and of doing them again, and better. I had worked on this piece for hours, thinking about the solace offered, during the second theme, by those notes threaded on a single breath, about the exact tempo of the march, about the precise texture of the lyrical passages. . . . It was a very good experience.

Yet I remember my hesitation when I heard the result on the CD. I was divided between two contradictory reactions. On the one hand, there was the intense thrill of hearing myself on a professionally recorded medium; all at once, the months and years of work, practicing, and research made sense. All of those hand movements, the vitality that you breathe into the piano and into the ink and paper score, degree after degree on the musical scale, step by step up the octaves, all of that labor you thought had vanished with the time and with the spent years comes together like magic. It exists! It's you, it's yours, it will be you years after you are gone—at the same time, you have given a stranger, someone who might not have been born yet, this piece by Rachmaninoff that you have loved so much.

On the other hand, once the thrill passed, I was seized by terror. I heard only the faults in the recording. I was horribly disappointed. I had hoped for so much! I was exultant at the moment I was playing, completely concentrated on the execution of the piece, and all the more passionate as I knew that there was a safety net beneath me—every passage that disappointed me could be replayed as often as I liked. Who could guess the secret joy of playing in unison with oneself in the extreme sophistication of a recording studio? Breathing slowly, calming that burning point in the spine, giving color to notes or simply seeking out those that appear to me when I listen to a recording: these are all good exercises. But in my inexperienced youth, what weight did they represent compared with my excitement?

"So, Hélène, what do you think?"

The sound engineer had handed me the definitive version of the CD. Amiably, from behind his beard, and above his round bon vivant's belly, he waited for my green light, my seal of approval. I met his gaze, my eyes nearly filled with tears. I was so terribly disappointed, so unsatisfied! I composed a radiant smile, pasted it on my lips, and after a nod of the head to simulate total satisfaction, I turned away.

It's really nothing special, I told myself. It was a piece that had been recorded so many times, and to have made another version that was so flat, so unaccomplished in its interpretation, that went nowhere and was played in no discernible style, was a disgrace!

The great importance that I had expected from it, to impress him, collapsed like a soufflé. "Well, so what?"—that was all the commentary that this work deserved. Fortunately, it had been agreed that the CD would not be released for another year, at an appropriate occasion. I prayed that it would get lost on some dusty shelves, and I coldly resolved never again to touch the score.

It took me four years—four years of purgatory—before I returned to Rachmaninoff. The opportunity came in the form of a concert with Vladimir Fedoseyev. I was not exactly happy about this reunion: I felt no particular desire to take up the score again, to ask myself once again whether the Second Concerto represented for Rachmaninoff a definitive break with the period of silence and depression that had preceded its composition, or whether it was simply an attempt at forgetting, a sudden burst but not one without relapses. . . . I worked, and worked some more; then, two days before the concert, the work appeared to me: luminous, other, clear. The line and the architecture were revealed in their entirety, with great coherence and an equally great sobriety—a trifle spartan, even if the word seems at odds with Sergei Rachmaninoff. With this vision, the flame I needed to interpret the piece, or any other piece of music, was relit, high, straight, and brilliant.

I like to remember this story in moments of doubt—it illustrates the dangers of works one grows up with. They run the risk of becoming ordinary items in your daily landscape. So when you take them up after a long absence, you have to pull yourself up to their level with an effort that is far more laborious than the first time. Forget about trying to avoid it: your performance will be swiftly punished. Admittedly, the work that begins is astonishing, almost strange—you must evaluate the distance that you have come since you first played it, and you must study and analyze this path, whether it concerns the development of the soul or pure playing technique. If you do it in complete honesty, this introspection will often reveal deformations, defects, and blind and deaf spots to which you may have fallen victim.

In any case, I was too disappointed with the result of this first recording to waste too much time on it. Angrily, I literally erased it from my mind; I say angrily, because anger was a state that frequently flooded me at that time.

I spent the summer that followed the recording session in the Alps, on vacation with my parents. This escape, far from Paris and the Conservatory, did me a world of good. Everything enchanted me and brought me back to my childhood: long hikes in the mountains, the occasional glimpse of a fawn in the dappled evening light beneath the towering black pines raised to the sky like hands in prayer, the tangled profusion of tall grass and wildflowers in paths redolent with odors, and the round sleep of woodchucks that I would surprise in the early morning. Everything, that is, but the fever of my unrequited, orphaned love, and the anger that I was sure would resurge on my return to Paris. An anger that had nothing to do with my dissatisfaction with the CD.

The Greeks associated music and singing with archery: "The bow twanged, and the string sang," as it says in *The Iliad.* And Ulysses tests the tension of his bow by touching the string. "It sang sweetly under his touch like the twittering of a swallow."

The Greeks also liked to illustrate the knowledge of what is just by the image of an arrow that strikes the target. Indeed, Apollo is "the one who strikes from afar." He expresses his divinity through his music and the tones from his lyre, penetrating and clear, luminous and free, because his music announces the reign—so full of meaning—of the just measure. Apollo does not seek the soul; he wants the mind.

And the song of Apollo, the most enlightened of all the gods, does not ascend like the dream of an intoxicated soul. It flies right to the heart of a clearly selected target: the truth. It flies with the greatest precision: it is the sign of his divinity. Divine wisdom composes the music of Apollo; thus, when it rings out, perfection is brought to the world and harmony along with it. With it also, chaos takes on shape, raging passions submit to the ordered regularity of measure, and opposites unite in agreement. Music is the weapon of Apollo that creates the rules, knows what is just, what is necessary, and what is to come: it educates us—we mortals.

In Apollo, the wolf-born god, it is the spirit of intuitive knowledge that greets us—a spirit that stands up to existence and the world, and with unequaled freedom.

Why was I angry? First, because Marc Bleuse, the new director of the National Conservatory of Music in Paris, had decided to promote contemporary music. This was not a bad thing in itself—on the contrary, musicians have a duty to care about music written by their contemporaries and pay a substantial amount of attention to it. But at the time, what did I care about the future of contemporary music? I wanted to learn, progress, redouble my efforts, and I still knew nothing of the major piano repertoire. I had other names in mind besides Stockhausen, Xenakis, and Ohana, but Marc Bleuse wanted to put his stamp on things, and "contemporary music" was his watchword. What's more, there were other ways to approach contemporary music—instead of leaping from Scarlatti to Stockhausen, they could have had us study Liszt's final compositions, and only then introduce us to Webern and Schoenberg.

As it was, we already had very little time to study the classics. Classes lasted an hour, and we had two programs to work on in order to prepare for the *prix*: Program A, centered on a classical or romantic work, and Program B, which involved a modern piece. One had to play extracts of each style in both programs: Scarlatti, the first movement of a sonata by Beethoven, the first movement of a sonata by Chopin, and a Debussy.

In addition, three weeks before the *prix* examination, a mandatory piece was chosen in a blind drawing from a repertoire that we had never studied. Each student ran off to study it. As you can imagine, preparing for the *prix* examination demanded a colossal effort on which the future of all of the students rested. The goal—may I remind you?—was to obtain a *premier prix*. Only those with the *premier prix* are allowed to continue on to the next level of studies, which lasts two years. During these two years, you are expected to take two hours of class per week, attend the master classes of invited artists, who spend three days in Paris, and at the end of each year take part in an international competition.

Thus, every minute of class was precious, and we could not afford to waste even a second. Imagine our dismay when we learned that during the half-hour of the program devoted to the examination, the administration had decided to devote ten minutes to contemporary music! I exploded! I was already so frustrated at not being able to play an entire sonata, at being allowed to interpret only a first movement! I worked in a perpetual rage, whipping myself into a frenzy.

And then came the day of the competition.

I am standing in front of two envelopes, a few steps from the piano, which gleams like the smile of a wolf in the half-light of the hall. To one side are the seven members of the jury. Seven individuals, but they are like one person to me. They are a single organism, undulating, feverish, predatory on the snaking line of chairs—a sort of Medusa with many heads, with a multitude of fingers armed with little notebooks and pencils waving in the air, half conductor's baton, half schoolchild's ruler. For a moment, I have the impression I am back in school: "Mademoiselle Grimaud, to the blackboard . . ."

I select an envelope. I catch myself thinking, "Do I have a preference?" and I unfold the paper before the response comes. My heart answers for me as it starts to beat faster: "Program B." For this program, I have chosen Opus 33 of the études of Rachmaninoff. I play with all my love for Rachmaninoff, as if I were Rachmaninoff playing his work for the first time, wanting with his entire being for it to be loved. I play intensely. It's over. I wait. I wait, and the jury gives its verdict. Five votes out of seven. It's good, it's actually very good, but I am insanely angry. Up to now, I have always passed my examinations and *prix* unanimously.

The dismay and the bitter disappointment on my face are so obvious that the two jurors who voted against me begin to justify their choice.

"You must understand, playing that piece at your age! There's no way of knowing if you have talent! It's still too early. Especially since you picked Rachmaninoff! If only you had played a great composer like Chopin."

"At fifteen, you're still not mature, and your talent is not yet confirmed. We've listened to any number of child prodigies who didn't amount to anything."

I was dumbstruck. What was there to say? I had drawn Program B. Program B was centered on a modern piece. I had thus chosen Rachmaninoff. I could have chosen Ravel or Debussy, of course, but would performing either of those composers have shed more light on my maturity and staying power? If I was too young, then why let me play? The inconsistency of the argument disgusted me. *Why not judge the color of my eyes*, I said to myself. Or my height, or my provincial background? What a laugh! What are you doing playing Rachmaninoff when you were brought up among the cicadas, with the syntactical singsong of Jean Giono and Marcel Pagnol?

Fury, fury.

You have your *premier prix*, my parents and friends told me. What are you complaining about?

At the Conservatory, they said, "She's insanely demanding." She's so difficult! Unyielding. But I had always been unyielding. "You have to learn to take it easy, Hélène." How many times had I heard that sentence? Especially at moments when I thought that many people's lives were far too easy, insipid . . . and often unclear.

"The most important thing is that you can go on to the examination for admission to the next level."

Granted, but who was part of the jury for the competition? One of the members of the jury who thought I was too young.

"I don't want to! They can go to hell, all of them! I refuse to play in front of imbeciles who impose completely arbitrary conditions on the candidates. Who think that maturity can be judged by the date on my birth certificate!"

I had my arguments—maturity comes at many ages. It comes after you progressively cross a series of thresholds: whether earlier or later, more or less spaced over time. We always have new experiences that are not necessarily linked to a chronological process. I laid out my arguments to the one I loved. I wanted him to understand their double meaning. I felt completely mature, annealed by the fire of passion.

He put forward his arguments. Learnedly. In my life I was going to meet dozens of imbeciles, or people that I thought were imbeciles. Would every one of them have the power to knock me off my path? Was I then capable of doing things exactly my way, according to my point of view, and incapable of doing them *for me*, only for me, with sufficient intensity as to hear nothing but the music that was to come?

Yes or no?

Two weeks later, I was unanimously admitted to the next level called the third cycle.

Love. Love of my fifteen years. Love that gave me the illusion that with you I had been born—love my beginning; and since I will not survive you—love my unimaginable end.

Love, no matter in what form you appear to us, no matter what your incarnation on this earth, in our world, it is you, immortal god, that we love the first time. You rose up like an apparition, a phantom that shimmers suddenly in the night, a luminous and intangible form that dressed my body with stars. I moved, I stirred the air, and as in summer's warm waters, beneath the moon, love lit my skin with the myriad nocturnal sparkling of the sea.

Love that my fifteen-year-old heart dressed up like a doll in the raiment of the moon, a coat of sun, and time's cape, clothes of a knight, of Apollo, like a magician, without knowing that the more one bedecks you, the more one takes away your mystery. But who cares? Love, incessant creation. "Perfect and reinvented measure, marvelous and unexpected reason," in the words of Rimbaud. You were my will made manifest. You made me understand that real life is not what comes to us, but what comes from us. I wanted to be. To love is to be. And it is far more a matter of creating one's life than of receiving it.

❦

What can I say about the two years that followed? They were a whirlwind, a time of much work, hopes, and smiles. The first of the two years were entirely devoted to music and to the piano, rigorously studying the obligatory coursework.

I did my homework diligently. I studied *Petrouchka*, the *Appassionata*, the *Waldstein*, *Gaspard de la Nuit*, and several sonatas by Scarlatti, one of which, in B minor, is to die for. It pulls at your heart and doesn't let up. I attended several workshops. I practiced, enormously. I felt that I was making progress, and there is nothing better than that to make you dizzy. I approached scores in a different way because I was more advanced, even if the approach remained essentially the same. The artistic director of the Orchestre de Paris, Pierre Vozlinsky, heard a broadcast of a recital at the Aix Festival and invited me to take part in MIDEM, the international music marketplace held annually in Cannes.

And then—above all, I should say—there was the chance, that twist of fate that allowed a crack to develop, a crack that was at first imperceptible, but which then snaked its way into my reality until an undeniable break took place.

By chance, I stumbled upon a brochure that extolled the splendor and the merits of the Tchaikovsky competition. Tchaikovsky, in Moscow! In the gray Paris winter and the cold February drizzle, these names resounded like a marching order. They shone like a gateway out of the daily routine. O Russia! Holy land, thrice holy, where the sky is clear, where the sun bedecks in diamonds and garnets the whole country—all of its ice and snow. There, the barometer announces the best weather in the world for nature. How I dreamed of Russia, white and red! Those plains, those birches, that wild, untamed forest, temple of priests and muzhiks, that intense compassion blossoming like an innocent flower on the faces of the most hardened criminals, as well as on the most innocent young girls, demons, and witches.

I was used to visiting Russia in my dreams, like a block of night, hard and cold. At the same time, this hardness, this cold, were like a baptism to me—misfortune itself had a presence that seemed beautiful, serene, fully approved of by the heart, and justifying it. How did I dream of Russia? Wrapped in leather, fitted out with a wealth of forests and mists. I thought of it as a drunken boat caught between the North Sea to the west, and the infinite shore of a never-ending East; a world within a world, with nothing mechanical about it. In this Elsewhere, I imagined that everything was directed toward love, toward excess, toward an intoxication of soul that surpassed the inebriation of the senses. I wandered through landscapes where the snow was a solid river, where winter is the underside of a time that has stopped, a time that keeps you beneath the lamplight, in a shadowy silence where fugitive forms have footsteps like phantoms. And, always, this richness of being, unheard of elsewhere: faith constructs life's horizon, overlaps its edges. It is its hope; it forms life's atmosphere, exactly like music.

I loved everything about Russia, without knowing anything about it: the varicolored domes of the Moscow churches, the izbas (log houses), and the dachas built of wood and stone that evoked the heroes of Chekhov and Turgenev. My soul shared the anxiety of these souls and their flames, alternately black and joyful. I knew nothing, but I already knew everything. I knew it from devouring the works of Dostoyevsky, from absorbing them into myself to the point where every word became a note of music, then a concerto, then a symphony in my soul, until—when I heard them for the first time—these works were given names and were revealed to me: Rachmaninoff, Scriabin, and Stravinsky, Rimsky-Korsakov, Prokofiev, and all of Shostakovich. I am sure, dear reader, that you also have had the experience of receiving, when you are reading, a sentence that seems as if it was written just for you.

"If my life had ended at that instant, I would have died joyfully," exclaimed Dostoyevsky.

These words made their way into my heart when I was barely fifteen years old. They became wedded to my soul, wrapping it in a thousand tender gestures. Thus, in rendezvous that were both amorous and passionate, I met Dostoyevsky for entire nights, hidden beneath my covers, with only a flashlight for illumination. In his novels, which I followed in the order of pages and the disorder of passages, thanks to his words, and guided by his very special art of ellipsis and parable, I affirmed that suffering is the source not of our desire, but of our certainty. By exposing eternally desperate hearts, Dostoyevsky showed me just how deep the love of life can go in profound beings born to suffer. A kind of love that leads to every excess, which elsewhere the law calls crimes.

Dostoyevsky suffered from the city; he suffered from solitude; he suffered from himself and from others. I resonated with all he said; I understood every nuance. But above all, I loved what this man was: sensitive to all life and all animals, with a just heart that did not play out a drama of passions. I saw him on the cross with them, and sometimes I saw myself there with him.

"After you, and please excuse our happiness," said Prince Myshkin, opening the door for a twenty-year-old wretch, racked with consumption and envy and about to die.

"Why do you humiliate yourself like this?" shouted the passionate young girl to the innocent prince. "Why have you no pride?"

And he, in response, as insensitive to vanities as to his demise: "What does my grief and my misfortune matter, if I am able to be happy?"

And Raskolnikov, the assassin, to the holy prostitute: "You, too, you have put yourself above the rules: you have destroyed a life, your own. It comes down to the same thing."

And: "I wanted to be daring: I killed. And it is myself I have slain."

And: "Jesus is with the animals before he is with us."

And: "If the judge were just, wouldn't the criminal perhaps be not guilty?"

And on and on. And many other words, many other sentences that force you to look at yourself, and that remind you of your own humanity.

Tolstoy was my other source. He gave me a family of intimate friends: Anna Karenina; Natasha and Prince Andrei; Nikolai of *Childhood* and *Youth*; but also Levin and his young wife; Ivan Ilyich, whose agony was so close to Tolstoy's own; the husband of the lover who was so enraged by the violin in "The Kreutzer Sonata" . . . In short, he showed me a Christ that required neither soothing caresses nor shameful hopes: a selfless soul, solitary, devoid of any corruption. A soul that is the very signature of the Russian soul. A soul driven to a peak of passion that offered me the breadth of the universe. This is the soul that I wanted to find in Moscow, playing Rachmaninoff, in this competition that fell into my life like a star. Ignore the omen? Madness! I ran at top speed to see my piano professor to ask him for the letter of recommendation—both necessary and indispensable—to register.

In a word: my enthusiasm fell on deaf ears. My suggestion provoked a long sigh, half dismay, half fatigue. Another whim! Bringing up the question of these international competitions again, when my professor had advised me to enter the Busoni competition, which had an excellent reputation, famous for the rigor of its jury and the honesty of its verdicts. In addition, he fully believed that I had already entered.

"Busoni, Busoni." This name awakened no echo of happiness, no enchanted worlds, no universe in tune with my own. I took his advice, and this is what I did with it: Busoni? Down the chute!

"I must absolutely enter the Tchaikovsky competition," I insisted.

"You aren't ready for that competition. You have too little of the required repertoire. You'll make yourself look ridiculous. In addition, I represent France on the jury. Therefore, I will have to abstain from voting."

Thus he could not give me the letter, just as he had thought it wise to not support me in working on a long piece at the beginning of the *mention* year. I was furious. I had only seconds to persuade him: the closing date for the competition was that very day. I understood that, at any rate, I would have little luck in changing his mind. But I could still prove to him that I was capable of doing it. Alone. By myself. Better than an adult.

I didn't say a word. I took my brochure and turned on my heel. Right into the office of my sight-reading teacher! He, at least, might encourage my daring.

A letter of recommendation? Yes, of course. And how shall we write it? On Conservatory letterhead, that would be best. I was certainly not going to contradict him! I could have kissed him! As for the letterhead, well, I had a stack of it in the file.

I only had to ask and the letter was written. Two minutes later, my open sesame was in an envelope with the registration forms duly filled out. And off it went into the letterbox!

Next stop, Moscow!

Since antiquity, the various peoples who have identified themselves with an ancestral wolf, or who have used it as a totem, have one thing in common: they have all been nomadic or rebellious peoples. In fact, although farmers and land dwellers saw the wolf as the ultimate unpredictable and dangerous hunter—a cattle thief and decimator of fat, tender game—warriors and people of the wind and open spaces were fascinated by the wolf for its intelligence and its tracking skills. Thus, the great nomadic conquering tribes, the Turks and Mongols, placed the wolf's image on their standards, as the Roman legions did when they set off to build their empire throughout Europe.

In his book *La Louve du Capitole* (The Capitoline She-Wolf), Jerôme Carcopino wrote, "In the first rank of the gods who protected invasions was Mamers, the Mars of the Latins, who later would sire Romulus and Remus and who would guide, in the third century B.C., a final Sabine migration from Campania to Messina. The hordes advanced under the sign of the god of battle, behind the attribute that was, to their eyes, his physical manifestation, the wolf, which led them to Beneventum and all the way to Lucania."

In pre-Roman Italy, three warrior tribes claimed the wolf as their founding ancestor. The Lucanians, as Pliny tells us, even called their leader Lucius after the name of the wolf-god, Apollo Lukeios, whom the Romans called Apollo Lucius. They stamped the effigy of this animal on their coins, three centuries before Christ, along with the word "Lukianon," as a reminder that their nation was directly descended from the wolf.

To the north of Rome, the Hirpi-Sorani, the "wolves of Sora," danced barefoot on hot coals twice a year, around their priests, in memory of the oracle who had saved them from death and defeat because he had advised them to "act like wolves."

In central Europe, the Hirpini venerated the wolf; their name means "those who belong to the wolf." Other tribes in western Europe called themselves by similar names: the Volci in what is now the Languedoc region of France, and the Veletes in eastern Europe whom their neighbors renamed Volki, "the wolves," because of their unbeatable ferocity.

In ancient Greece, illustrious figures added this glorious epithet to their name. Thus we read about the Spartan legislator Lycurgus, "the one who leads the wolf"; a king of Nemea also called Lycurgus; and a third Lycurgus, an Athenian orator from the fourth century B.C. Then there is Lykos, the grandson of Tantalus.

According to the Greek historian Diodorus of Sicily, Macedon, the great hero of Macedonia, wore a wolf's head on great occasions. And there's more. According to Herodotus, certain Scythians who had proven to be particularly valiant or fierce warriors were granted by the gods the privilege of changing into wolves several days each year.

The first knights of the Christian West were not immune to this fascination. Many of them gave the wolf's effigy the place of honor on their armor. It is part of the coat of arms of twelve hundred French families.

Alas! The glorious conquests end and nature loses its mysteries. Fairies, elves, nymphs, centaurs, and unicorns were driven away. Men shut the door to Eden and threw away the key. As for the Olympian gods, they were served with an eviction notice. They went into exile . . . but where? Only the wolves, the accursed wolves—declared dangerous and demonic as more and more towns appeared—mourn them and call to them some nights beneath the moon.

Six

At last I was in Moscow. I had dreamed of snow on Red Square; instead, I was suffocating in the heat. It was the month of June, and the entire city was bathed in monsoonlike humidity, an incandescence that made the idea of a cataclysm seem imminent. My mother had come with me on this journey, which had been made in spite of everyone. We had just stepped out of the shuttle bus that connected the airport with the hotel. We were both in a state of dazed bewilderment, not a lag made of hours, but a physical lag between body and spirit. In our minds, both of us were still immersed in our daily routine. *Normally, at this time of day, I* . . . But there was no more "normally," only discovery and the necessary adaptation. In addition to getting into the competition program, it was a matter of learning the rules, getting used to the landscape, to the city, and observing the customs of these Muscovites we met in the streets so that we could better understand them. Tired by the journey, stunned by the heat, we needed all the swishing softness of the Russian language; needed the incredible Cyrillic alphabet, which transforms street signs into hieroglyphics; needed the enormous grid of their avenues and the sad Cubism of their buildings to confirm the reality of our presence there. We smiled at each other to express our joy at this discovery.

I was radiant with joy as I rarely was. As soon as I set foot on Russian soil, I felt strangely at ease. It was difficult to explain this feeling of well-being. For example, if I had thought of the immense distance that separated the city from the sea—as I sometimes amused myself in doing when I felt hemmed in, conjuring up in my imagination the houses, the suburbs, the new little urban clusters, and then the increasingly present countryside, then leaping over bridges, rivers, and forests, snaking my way up mountains that slowed my progress, all those many kilometers domesticated by human beings, all those spaces tamed and brought to heel—if I had thought of all that distance, I should have suffocated. I have always needed to live near water, a river at least, with the idea that the sea is only a few hours away. A river, a stream, a spring, so that I can always be within earshot of living water, *legato, rubato,* its ungraspable curves like a snake's slow, incandescent green undulations in the grass, whose elegance is never sufficiently extolled. The snake and the river—at once slow and strong, winding and straight, fluid and rebellious. Water close to my life is like a suitcase that is always ready to go, like an open airline ticket at the bottom of my bag—a powerful freedom. In Hindustan, did you know that the servant in charge of keeping the house cool by wetting the floors is called "the heavenly one"? And that, even today, the fishermen who descended from the conquistadors still scour the remote regions of the Bahamas where the Fountain of Youth is said to bubble to the surface—in search of which their ancestors joyfully set forth, joyfully meeting their deaths?

In Moscow—a capital landlocked within its fields, its vast republics, its steppes and its tundra, its lakes and birch forests, where many a poet lost his way, and where Tolstoy no doubt disappeared one winter night, alone on horseback and near death—all of this should have suffocated me. And yet I was, despite all this, well. Then suddenly, luminously, I knew why. For the first time in my life, the feeling of being elsewhere, in transit, passing through, had left me.

"Perhaps I'm imagining things," I told my mother as we climbed on a bus, "but I'm sure that I lived here in another life."

"In another life, or an inner life?" she joked.

Then, in a serious tone: "I believe you if you say so. I believe in these feelings of déjà vu. Gérard de Nerval wrote some beautiful poems on the subject, you know."

She recited one to me, whose verses spoke of an old château made of brick, and a park with forlorn statues. I looked at her, energetic despite the heat wave, and in that moment I understood, like a revelation, that I would never again live in Aix-en-Provence, that I had to leave because I would never be "happy" there—if indeed that word had any meaning for me at the time. This was a fleeting thought, as wrenching as a farewell, as when you look at a person and know in a flash that he or she will die. I would no longer be exclusively her daughter. It was over. I was taking flight.

I had the absurd desire to say the word "mama" in a loud voice.

Mama, my delicious mama. Song of my childhood. She faced life with a powerful yet modest courage. She listened to me, nodding. Took me in her arms, calming me . . . Mama, who was always worried for me, her "unpredictable" daughter.

On the plane that carried us both to Moscow, I told her that the mad love I had nourished for more than two years had finally triumphed. I had known the strength and the softness of his arms. I announced my conquest in typical fashion: abruptly, disjointedly, my mind already focused on the present, the competition, and the repertoire into which I had thrown myself like a wild wind through a tunnel—learning in a topsy-turvy fashion and feverishly devouring scores night and day.

For a moment she had closed her eyes and hesitated, but then had pulled herself together and made no comment. I understood the struggle raging inside her: her little girl, her Nanou, her child, the one who had always embraced life like an athlete, wrestling and rolling, was becoming a woman. The little girl with the perpetually skinned knees who threw her arms around any animal that showed her affection, who dreamed of becoming a veterinarian and living in a zoo, or perhaps a lawyer, defending lost causes or writing wrongs in order to restore justice to the world—now her little girl was talking to her about love, like every other girl her age in the world.

I was one step closer to the open sea—an unknown sea where no one could be sure of the sailing conditions. I understood her interior struggle without realizing the worry that I had put in her heart; who, at sixteen, understands a mother's anxiety? And then, we were together in Moscow, weren't we? I instinctively rediscovered the old understanding that had always been our bond. She was still the only one with whom I loved to talk, and above all laugh—laugh as I hadn't laughed for months in Paris. On top of it, here in Moscow, everything became a pretext for our uncontrollable fits of laughter.

For one thing, the horrific logistics of the competition. They were the worst I had ever encountered; it was as if Kafka and Alfred Jarry had planned them together. The most important moments for the contestants coincided exactly with mealtimes. The choice was certainly a drastic one—between inspiration and a hot lunch. I was only half prepared, and whenever I had a moment, I went to the practice rooms we had been assigned. Two out of three times, they were being used for regular lessons, which had not been canceled. I thus began wandering through the enormous buildings of Moscow's music world, looking for a piano and a quiet place to work. I met other lost contestants, as well as a number of young Russians, equally confused, looking for their regular classes. While walking down a corridor, one heard here and there clumsy scales laboriously being picked out by the fingers of young students, as well as some truly marvelous performances. It was in this way that I had the shock of hearing Roger Muraro play his extraordinary version of the *Hammerklavier* Sonata.

I was forced to admit—and it was infuriating!—that my entourage had been right. My level wasn't high enough; I was stumbling through the repertoire. But what did it matter? I was joyful; I observed, like an entomologist observing his insects, the struggles between the competing musicians, the false smiles and the low blows, as well as moments of great generosity. Some took a perverse pleasure in attending others' presentations, swelling the ranks of listeners with their hostile presence. They gave off such fear of another's triumph, so much jealousy, that one could feel the waves of it all throughout the hall. Others threw all of their support behind a new friend, and it was a lovely sight to see them in the audience playing along in spirit, miming the movements of body, hands, and fingers, like mothers who open their mouths at the same time as their babies at feeding time.

And then, during those days that in my memory are continually filled with sunlight, there were passionate conversations with young Russians, who spoke to me of their hopes, of what music brought to their lives, lives made particularly difficult by the political and economic realities of the time. They were very giving, and I found in them that generosity of nature and grandeur of spirit that I had dreamed of for so long.

I spent the last two evenings before our departure from Moscow walking through the streets alone. Or rather, I was accompanied by my thoughts. I felt well. Really well. I was filled with a delicious feeling of solitude. I was far from the Conservatory and far from home! I experienced this in all of its sweetness. And then, where was home after all? Why not here, alone?

> *O solitude, my sweetest choice!*
> *Places devoted to the night,*
> *Remote from tumult, and from noise,*
> *How ye my restless thoughts delight!*
>
> *O, how I solitude adore,*
> *That element of noblest wit,*

Where I have learnt Apollo's lore,
Without the pains to study it . . .

These lines were written by the poet Katherine Philips. Henry Purcell put them to music in one of his most beautiful songs. I sang them to myself, cherishing the idea of never returning to Paris. I shivered with pleasure.

I won nothing in Moscow. I was awarded no prize.

My professors were right to fear the consequences for me. In Moscow, for the first time, the idea of a solitary path took root in my mind, along with the need to flee far away, high up, to find my way on my own.

❦

Like the fox, the wolf (*Canis lupus*) is a member of the Canidae family. Members of this family have five toes on each forefoot, forty-two teeth, and an elongated muzzle. Along with the domestic dog, the jackal, and the coyote, it forms the *Canis* genus, characterized by a pronounced forehead, a somewhat shorter tail, and a less pointed muzzle.

The wolf measures about 55 inches long, the tail adding 12 to 20 inches to this. Its weight ranges between 60 and 180 pounds, and it can stand as high as three feet at the withers, but usually several inches less. The tail is straight and carried straight out and in line with the body. At the base of the tail, a scent gland secretes a specific smell at mating time. The pupils are round. The ears are pointed and erect, and the neck is large and thick. The carnassial teeth are extremely powerful and are of standard shape. Not only are the canines extremely long, but they are very solidly embedded in the jaw; the incisors are well developed. Wolf coats vary considerably in both thickness and color. The quality of the fur is determined by the region where the wolf lives. For example, in Nordic countries the fur is long, thick, and abundant. The belly, neck, and thighs are particularly covered in fur. In more temperate climates, the fur is shorter and less silky. The most common color for wolves is fawn mixed with black. This is lighter on the underside of the body, and appears redder in the summer and more yellowish in winter. The very specific shape of the rib cage powers the animal's most common gait—a trot—and allows for an impressive ventilation of the lungs. Although the wolf is not very fast—its top speed does not exceed thirty miles an hour—it is particularly resistant to fatigue: it captures its prey through endurance. There is the famous case of a wolf that was released for hunting by the Dauphin at Versailles in the seventeenth century: it was finally captured three days later in Rennes, about 180 miles away, after many changes of horses and dogs. The wolf's powerful jaws and forequarters allow it to run with a ewe in its mouth, and to drag for miles a trap in which its leg has been caught.

The male wolf reaches full maturity at age four. Life expectancy is fifteen years, an age rarely attained, as it is a tough existence for wolves out there.

The geographic distribution of the wolf includes part of Europe, parts of Asia, and North America. It is not found in Africa, South America, or Australia. The species is thus geographically widespread—there are still several packs in the Apennines in Italy, and in the Spanish Sierra Nevada—yet its range areas are constantly shrinking. The wolf can adapt to all types of habitats—mountains and plains, forests and steppes, arid zones and marshlands—provided the areas are not too heavily populated.

Wolves are eminently social creatures, and they form families and even larger packs in order to survive and to hunt. Where wolves are found in the lower forty-eight United States, these groups contain between four and eight animals, with a record twenty wolves in a pack in Yellowstone Park. In Canada, packs can contain as many as thirty wolves. Starting in the autumn, wolf pups follow the adults as they hunt. The nightly howling of wolves is a call to assemble, an invitation to join the pack.

The larger the game, the larger the pack. Pack function has a specific social arrangement and a perfectly established hierarchy. A ritual of body postures—submission, threat, challenge—designates each wolf's place in the hierarchy.

Each pack consists of a dominant wolf couple—the alpha wolves—and young wolves born in previous springtimes, who are beneath them. The alpha couple decides the time and place that hunting will occur. During mating season wolves can engage in choreographed combat without killing each other: the defeated wolf shows submission by baring his throat to the victor, thus deflecting aggression.

All ethologists recognize that, contrary to the legend, the wolf is more cunning than the fox. It is particularly intelligent, cautious, and very patient.

❧

It was September, with its strange mixture of bustle and nostalgia, full of projects for the school year, and full of sadness for the summer that was nearing its end. I was back in class at the Conservatory and working, but since Moscow a revolution had started inside me. I was haunted by the idea of pursuing my solitary way. I listened, albeit distractedly. I looked, but now there was always that large crack in the edifice, undermining the very foundations of my world. I was almost seventeen. Was I "not serious," as Rimbaud wrote? I never really understood what this term meant. They called me fanciful and bizarre. Yes? So what? I was above all determined to carve out my own personal path in both life and music.

I knew that I had always benefited from wonderful professors, who put me back on the right track whenever I lost my way in an interpretation. I was not questioning this guidance; I just wanted with all my might to study an entire work, to approach it anew, and to be able to play it by expressing myself with it, through it— and without having it spoon-fed to me.

I wanted to use what I knew, to confront the music one-on-one, to build my own personal laboratory of notes and intuitions in order to perform my own experiments, and to discover at last what sort of dialogue I was capable of having with the great works. I could have waited for the end of the third cycle and the benediction of an international competition to bring my education to a glorious finish. But I was in a hurry. I started to develop a genuine passion for the straight path—direct style and direct language. Wait? Why should I wait? To suppress my desires?

A part of my desires, of my soul, was wearing "seven-league boots." Oh, to make that leap! To fly! To spread my wings! To take flight, even though there was still much to learn, and even if I was learning a great deal—the second year had been very difficult.

Of course, staying on had its advantages: I wouldn't have to think, since I never had to think for myself. All I had to do was work on the scores as they were presented. When I came across a pitfall, someone would show me how to avoid it. My apprenticeship followed a wisely laid-out gradation of difficulties. I advanced across terrain that was tended just for me, along a path bordered by perfectly trimmed hedges and scattered with rose petals, without one single pebble to slip into my shoe. This finicky, meticulous supervision was stifling me.

And him, the one I had loved so. He had that part of me that I had given to him, and he had plans for her. Did he want to tie her down to that place, to his life, to an orderly daily routine? I realized that I had to leave him, that I had to reclaim, to regroup, to *recompose* myself. I also realized that I could do it. "We have faith in poison. We know how to give our whole life each day."

"I'm going to leave the Conservatory."

"Look, that's just not possible. Musicians work with their professors until they're at least twenty-five, and sometimes longer. And you, you think that by yourself, when you're barely seventeen . . . With less than ten years of piano behind you? What will become of you? You'll lose everything!"

What strange arguments! I know musicians who live with this

fear: "Oh, but if something happened to me tomorrow, if I could no longer play, if I lost an arm, what would I do?" Me, I know exactly what I would do. Earn less money? What does it matter, as long as I'm enjoying myself and maintaining my lifestyle? I don't need much. A beautiful house, a pool, lovely things, a nice car—none of that interests me. And anyway, what was I supposed to be afraid of? Living?

Fear, always fear, the withdrawal into oneself, the safety net. We need a much stronger motivation than fear to change the world and make it a better place. We need beauty, love, and even risk.

How could I explain to those people who, with the best intentions in the world, advised me to be so careful? "Behave yourself. Be patient. Be nice."

"If you don't get it immediately, you'll never get it," someone said to me one day. A round of applause, please—the important things cannot be taught. Culture, knowledge, and study are edifying, but not enlightening. Everything had to be lived. Everything was still behind the door. All I had to do was open it, slip across the threshold, and close it behind me.

The grievances I had with the Conservatory (which I will always remember because sometimes even I thought I was harping) were mostly about repertoire. I wanted to play Brahms. They tried to talk me out of it.

"You don't have the experience. You play Chopin so much better. Why don't you perfect the study of his works? And for Brahms, you know, you need to have been around the block a bit."

I couldn't stop myself. I read scores. Brahms's life, his notes, studies and analyses, and then more scores. Nothing about Brahms seemed strange or unknown to me. So I closed my eyes and tried to understand what I was lacking that they tried to keep me away from this composer. I found nothing. I reread a concerto. A profound, deep-rooted attraction rose up in me, a feeling of familiarity. I surrounded myself with Brahms. Books about his life lay all about me. I loved leaving a volume of his works on my piano. I would sometimes look at it a long time. Then, without taking my eyes from it, I would slowly back away and contemplate at length the music stand, the stool where I sat, and the open keyboard. This simple perspective filled me with happiness and a sense of rightness.

As soon as I heard a work by Brahms, or a student at the Conservatory working on one of his pieces, I had a sense of *recognition*. It was very bizarre—the feeling that something had been written for you, and that this something corresponded exactly to the fluctuations of your emotions. I felt that I was rediscovering the works, although I had never played them or even heard them previously. This incredible feeling of familiarity never left me, the sense of something close to me, made for me.

I think that I play Chopin fairly well, but I never reached the same degree of intimacy with him that I did with Brahms. He immediately occupied an unshakable place in my heart. At that time, some other composers left me completely cold. Perhaps that would change, but the Romantic repertoire has always enchanted me; at sixteen, I was drawn to it like a magnet.

I am often told that an artist should perform everything. What a curious idea! Are we machines? How is it possible that an artist, a real artist, would have the same amount to say, and at the same moment, about Mozart and Debussy, or about Bach and Chopin? Is it conceivable that someone could be entirely focused on the world of Brahms and at the same time be on intimate terms with a completely different universe? I can't imagine it, unless that person is missing something in the deepest core of his or her personality.

What I loved so profoundly in the music of Brahms is what it describes, note after note: a life voluntarily lived apart and devoted exclusively to the essential. And what is this music, if not the story of an awaited traveler, always the same, always another, who has set off standing on the deck of a ship, standing at the bow facing the sun, for a journey from which there is no return? This traveler is Brahms himself, a being who never surrendered. I loved his impetuous character, his torment and his furies, the emotional heartbreak and the relationship to the world he expressed so subtly in his contrapuntal music. In German, his name means "heather," and like heather in a dry landscape, Johannes Brahms was born fiery, violent, sensual, and passionate.

As a young man he was beautiful, as only geniuses know how to be—by acknowledging their deep inner life. He had eyes like slate after rain, with eyelids that enshrined the pale light of his gaze. His mouth was calm and virginal, with a shadow of a smile that reinforced the melancholy of his blond face, by turns enthusiastic and taciturn.

And such passion! Johannes Brahms's great voyage began on September 30, 1853. He was twenty years old. He knocked at the door of a house in Düsseldorf. It was opened by a child whose parents were the celebrated musicians Robert and Clara Schumann.

Brahms had brought with him the Sonata in C, his latest manuscript. Schumann was used to this sort of visit. He received the young musician politely, but spoke barely a word. He simply invited him to take a seat at the piano. Brahms complied: scarcely had he finished the first movement of his piece than Schumann rose to his feet, enthusiastic. He called his wife, saying: "Come here! You will hear a music that you have never heard before." And to Brahms: "Young man, please begin again." The next day, October 1, Schumann wrote a single line in his diary: "Visit by Brahms. A genius."

And what was the result of this encounter? A love affair among the three. It was an intense, lucid, and very special relationship— no doubt it was Schumann who loved the other two the most. The pain bordering on ecstasy that one hears in Brahms's music, what is it if not the music of a pure love, the purest and most blinding love? An impossible love.

Brahms composes the way a sublime shooting star writes its dizzying arc: he is bound to nothing, and answers to no demand. If he finds an impediment in his way, he smashes it and returns to his heavenly abysses. At the piano, in his last works, he reveals chords that are, quite simply, tragic. And what does it matter if, having loved Clara, he wanted to marry her daughter Julie? She alone would have been able to offer him the love of his two friends by giving him children. His notes were his only children.

❧

Since the beginning of time, man has dreamed of his double. This idea, suggested and nourished by mirrors, springs, and lakes, amplified by the birth of identical twins, has never ceased to flourish in the various cultures of the world. Pythagoras saw it in the shape of a loved one: "A friend is another self." Plato imagined it within our-selves, a shadow being that mutely moves us, and whose existence we must be aware of and acknowledge. Socrates' motto "Know thy-self," carved in the pediment of the temple of Apollo at Delphi, al-luded to exactly this notion. In myth and fable, the double comes looking for humans in order to lead them off to their deaths. For example, the *Doppelgänger* appeared in Germany; in Scotland this creature was the "fetch." Edgar Allan Poe created William Wilson, whose double was his conscience, which ended up killing him and dying in turn. Dostoyevsky explored this idea a great deal: it haunts nearly all of his works, triumphing in *The Brothers Karamazov.*

Robert Louis Stevenson explores this concept endlessly in his work. *The Strange Case of Dr. Jekyll and Mr. Hyde,* his most famous story, tells the story of how a gentle but overly curious man uses a potion to bring forth his double, a doubling that for him proves fatal. But in his epic poem *Ticonderoga,* Stevenson recounts the tragic legend that best explains the concept of coming face-to-face with this other self, which is the sign that death is imminent.

For my part, the idea of a double has inhabited me since child-hood. First it was a geographic double: a place that would be not my own, but me. A double I have always wanted to meet, and that I sometimes thought I'd found in certain composers such as Brahms. I like the idea of this twin, in the way that Yeats described it, for whom our double is our reverse side, our contrary and complement—the one who we are not and will never be. Yet this is the one I sometimes meet in concerts, in magic moments when the interpretation is consummate. As Helen of Troy says in Goethe's *Faust*: "Singly I troubled the world, doubly more so."

But of all these approaches, it is the Jewish one I prefer. For the Jews, the appearance of the double is not the sign of imminent death but rather the assurance that one has achieved a prophetic state.

Even more marvelously, Talmudic tradition tells the story of a man in search of God who ends up face-to-face with himself.

❧

And so it came about that one morning I left the Conservatory. I turned my back on it, deserting my classes. I went back to Aix, back to my parents' house.

I knew what I wanted: solitude. To spread my wings, alone. But how? I didn't really know. I withdrew into myself, into my room, among my scores. I read them all day, agitated, floundering. They appeared to me like a life preserver rising up on the crest of a wave during a storm. Work; find the way. I worked by trial and error. I was on fire, and had no fear of failure. And yet ... if I had thought about what my chances were, I would have calculated them at exactly zero. Whom could I ask to listen to me without the seal of approval of the Conservatory, of a completed course of study, without the supervision of a professor? And why would anyone listen to me? A concert? What madness! I was really the only one who knew that I had a common destiny with music. Fortunately, I didn't ask myself any questions of this sort. I worked as I had never worked before or since.

As for my parents, were they perhaps relieved? If the adventure had to end, then let it end now, they told themselves. Now, before

I was too caught up, unfit for any other form of life than music, and therefore embittered, defeated, and sad. They had always feared my sudden swings of mood and taste, my compulsions and my abrupt dislike for something, my renunciations. If this latest passion had to die, then let it die right here and now.

Happily, my lucky star was still somehow shining high above me, and good luck, that fantastical little spirit, was with me. An extraordinary opportunity, which came about, as is often the case, due to an amazing coincidence. And one that came at the right moment.

If things present themselves when one is not ready, then nothing works. But there are those who are ready their whole lives, and for whom things never happen. For me, they happened at the right place and the right time. I had left the Conservatory, and now everything was finally going to begin!

You have no doubt also felt that feeling of déjà vu, the feeling that you have met someone or something before, the way I felt in Moscow—the feeling of a previous life. Do you also dream dreams, those dreams that reality will later describe as "premonitory"? Do you dream of a life to come?

That night I had a strange dream, one that would return often. I was myself, but at the same time hidden like a tortoise shut up in his shell. I had pulled back into a space that was my own, and from which I could barely hear the sound of the world—only a whisper, nothing more. I walked heavily, with a leaden step. I was suffocating somewhat. I could not understand why I had shut my-self in this shell, where I felt so marvelously well. Before me, the countryside was filled with the color of flowers, with wind and rain. It was a landscape that was entirely unknown to me, but apparently one in which I had created a large clearing, an enclosure in the midst of a dense forest. I walked toward the horizon, sur-rounded by a primeval landscape of intensely green grass, tossed by a great wind. I wandered completely alone in this vast space. My face was burned and caressed by the spindrift from an ocean whose roar I could hear, and which broke against a stubborn and resistant coastline, bony and gray, where landmasses jutting sea-ward kept watch for whales. And then suddenly I heard a long howl, an immense and absolutely vertical wail that filled me not with terror but with joy, as if finally by this call, what I was seek-ing was showing me the path in order to find it.

Each time I had this dream, I woke up at the precise moment of this howling, as if that land, stripped of its skin of earth, down to rock, had given its voice to this unknown being whose wail pen-etrated my every sense.

I woke at this briefly glimpsed, fleeting, and intangible vision. At the threshold of nights to come, I often prayed to heaven that the dream would return and bring with it the key to its meaning.

I no longer went to classes, but like all students in the second year of the third cycle, I had enrolled in master classes. Leon Fleisher was in Paris to give one. Fleisher, a pianist and conductor, was on the faculty of the Baltimore Conservatory and was considered one of the best piano professors in the world. Above all, he taught music. I heard nothing but superlatives about him. A brilliant and charismatic teacher, Leon Fleisher had always been obsessed with a question that troubled me as well: melodic continuity, so difficult for a pianist to execute. He had a theory about it, and a perfectly justified one: "Music is a horizontal force that unfolds in time." I had experienced this force physically the day I held a cello in my arms at the Aix Conservatory. The contact was so strong that it nearly proved fatal for my piano studies. It was like boarding a ship, taking hold of the rudder and, at the same time, with successive strokes of the bow, lashing forceful waves against it. It was extraordinarily sensual, and Leon Fleisher was quite correct when he added to his theory: "In the case of bowed instruments, the musician's movement is horizontal; he or she is in sync with the music. It is the same for wind instruments. The pianist's problem is that the action is exclusively vertical. This is the permanent challenge that we face in our art."

The other reason I would not have missed this class under any circumstance was Brahms, always Brahms. Leon Fleisher had recorded the composer's two concertos, as well as the Sixteen Waltzes (Opus 39), and *Variations on a Theme from Handel,* with breathtaking brio. He had the key, and I wanted it too. I wanted to understand how, by what magic, he had found the connection between the overall form and the details, and how both played a role in the fluidity of the interpretation.

The night before the master class, he gave a concert: the *Concerto for the Left Hand* by Ravel, directed by Daniel Barenboim. I rushed to this concert, and I listened as hard as I could, attentive yet filled with wonder. I physically understood his extraordinary vision of the work as a whole, based—not just on technique—but on his unequaled mastery of sound and discourse that carried all of the orchestra's musicians with him in his brilliance.

The next day, I was first in line in front of the doors to the master class. I should say right off the bat that as soon as I understood it, I detested the principle of these courses. I was appalled by the fake dialogue that took place between the young musician at the piano and the Master who addresses him or her, essentially to be heard by the other students. There was something false about it, something prearranged, theatrical, and condescending that bothered me enormously.

But now it was my turn to play. I played the first movement of Schumann's Sonata in F Sharp. As the echo of the last note faded away, I lifted my gaze to Leon Fleisher. Behind the square lenses of his eyeglasses, his expression was inscrutable. I did not look away. I waited.

"Do you think the piano should sound like a piano or like an orchestra?" he asked me abruptly, and in a loud voice so that everyone could hear—but I understood that only later.

He could have slapped me, and the effect would not have been any more disastrous. Why had he asked me that question? There was not a single ounce of my being that was not convinced of the answer. Of course, the piano *should* sound like an orchestra. I was all the more annoyed since, as far as I could see, I had no choice in my answer: he had asked me this question so that I would respond exactly as he wished. Not only had he noted my work, but he was using it to teach his course. What did he think? That I would blush, lower my gaze, and say, "Oh yes, Monsieur, the piano should . . ."?

"Last night, when you played Ravel's *Concerto for the Left Hand*, you had more colors in your playing than the entire orchestra."

Not one word more. Not the bat of an eyelid. He had asked me a question? I gave him the exact right answer. A well-played piano is just that: more color and timbre in its sonority than the entire orchestra, and as much richness as the pianist can offer it in terms of variety.

Leon Fleisher looked at me and muttered into his beard: "Don't embarrass me."

I was ready for everything, except these words. I was flabbergasted, unable to tear my gaze from his face, from his little beard, with that sentence in my head. How could a professor of his caliber and reputation take as flattery a remark that was simply about piano playing?

And how should I answer in turn? Nothing. I withdrew into my shell. I finished my lesson. And when, several months later, Daniel Barenboim advised me to go work with Fleisher in Baltimore, my reaction was swift and stubborn.

"No."

The incident did not lessen my admiration for him, for the extraordinary energy that his playing gave off, for his almost tangible musical intensity. But the answer was no. I wanted to do it alone. Completely alone. To be independent.

If Leon Fleisher had been God Himself, I would have refused just the same. It didn't matter how Daniel Barenboim suggested that I go to Baltimore that day—and just where were my parents going to find the money, on top of it all?—my refusal would have been just as definite.

I saw Leon Fleisher again two months later during another master class. I had understood and accepted the system, even though it continued to displease me just as much. Did he remember me? He gave no sign—neither amusement nor consternation—that he recalled our first encounter. But no teaching was ever more productive than what I learned that day. All at once, with just a few images, he made me understand the architecture of a piece and its importance, the directive force of the overall line. Among other great and beautiful things, he taught me "a pianist is an architect who uses rhythm as a basic building block."

At the end of the lesson, he said to me: "Whatever you do, you have the potential to do it very well on your own. Just remember, don't start too quickly. Perform as little as possible. Stay on the sidelines until you have found your own system."

He shook my hand and added: "I hear that you want to continue alone. It is a completely admirable undertaking, and you have everything it takes to make a success of it. Go to it."

Seven

In 1920, in the little village of Midnapore south of Calcutta, the villagers were frightened. There were spirits in the forest, beings who were half human, half animal—possibly sorcerers— who walked on all fours. Clearly, they sought to lay a curse on the village and to bring down every sort of plague on it. The few men who still dared to venture to the edge of this deep forest had no shortage of stories to tell. The others trembled, prayed, and tried to ward off bad fortune. When the Reverend J. A. L. Singh, on an evangelizing tour of this remote province, entered the village, he found its population prostrate and frozen with fear. All he heard about was sorcery and other demonic things. Finally, after a full two hours of discussion, he managed to get the beginning of an explanation. Two more hours were needed before the bravest hunters in the village agreed to accompany him to the places where these apparitions supposedly had been seen.

The little party set off in the afternoon and, after some discussion as to the exact location of the phenomenon, settled down to wait. And indeed, as night fell, as if they had emerged from the belly of the earth, three wolves appeared, followed by two wolf pups. Finally, bringing up the rear and walking on all fours, were two thin and disheveled creatures, their eyes gleaming. They growled like the wolves and followed in their tracks. The hunters were seized with terror at the sight of them and ran away shrieking. Neither promises nor threats by the Reverend Singh could persuade them to return to the spot that night or at any time thereafter.

A week later, on October 9, 1920, J. A. L. Singh returned to Midnapore, accompanied by a small army of men recruited from another village. He wanted to get to the bottom of the matter and to discover to which species the two animals he had glimpsed belonged.

An ambush was laid, and as happened the first time, everyone settled down to wait. The wolves finally appeared, then the wolf pups, followed by the creatures. The spears and nets were ready. The hunters attacked. Their orders were simple: catch the unidentified beasts alive, and without hurting them. They did not reckon on the she-wolf that, fangs bared, protected her young. The struggle was fierce, and the she-wolf had to be killed in order to capture the intended prey.

In the moment, the Reverend Singh could not evaluate the nature of his catch. The night was black and the party had to return to the encampment. It was there, in the light of a fire, that he understood what he had just ensnared—they were neither strange beasts nor sorcerers nor evil spirits, but two children. Not normal children, of course, not like those who played in the neighboring villages. They were two little humans, admittedly, but their posture and behavior belonged entirely to the world of wolves. Two little girls, in fact. One appeared to be barely two years old, the other eight. They were taken to the orphanage in Midnapore, where they were baptized: the younger one was called Amala, the older Kamala. Every day, in his personal diary, J. A. L. Singh noted the girls' activities and progress. He visited them and observed them closely. Amala survived not even another year, and died on September 21, 1921. Kamala lived for another nine years, dying at age seventeen.

When the reverend discovered them, the two girls were incapable of standing upright or speaking. Yet they could move on all fours at a phenomenal speed. They ate raw meat and, when night fell, warbled "a lovely babble of resounding notes, very high and piercing," as Singh noted in his diary. In addition, they had a particularly keen sense of smell and highly developed vision, particularly night vision. During the day, they clearly preferred the night. While Amala lived, the two children slept on top of each other, entwined, as in a wolf's den. When Amala died, Kamala refused to eat or drink for three days, sniffing the places where her little companion used to go and spend time.

For the first six years of her life among human beings, Kamala could not stand to wear the clothes they tried to put on her; she never used her hands to eat meat, and as soon as she wanted to run, she dropped to all fours. In addition, she refused to be washed, unless she was held under water by force, and she never ate the least bit of vegetable matter. It took six years for her to finally understand and to be able to mutter about forty words, for her biological rhythm to become aligned with that of her fellow humans—sleeping at night, the night that she came to fear, by the way—and for her to learn to eat with her hands and at set meal-times, and to drink from a glass.

The scientific community was fascinated with the case of Kamala and Amala, the wolf-children of Midnapore—it finally shed new light on the behavior of wolves, which were said to be incapable of raising a human child, unlike monkeys. This thesis was based on strictly biological observations: a she-wolf suckles her young for two months, then feeds them regurgitated meat. When they are four months old, pups follow their parents in order to hunt with them. What would become of a child left behind in the den? The lair is often abandoned as soon as the pups can get about on their own.

In fact, a she-wolf can suckle its young up to the age of four months. She then has no more milk but can regurgitate predigested meat that the stomachs of four-month-old babies would be able to digest. A she-wolf's maternal instinct is no doubt strong enough to force her to return to the lair to feed those of her natural, or adopted, young that need her. In addition, the wolves that raised the two girls in Midnapore did not belong to the same subspecies as European or American wolves. Indian wolves are less threatened by humans; the Indian climate is milder, and they are protected under the tenets of Hinduism, the predominant religion of those with whom they share territory. Where else but in India could Kipling have written the story of Mowgli?

In retrospect, I have the impression that the summer that followed the encounter with Leon Fleisher and my departure from the Conservatory was the monsoon season. Every stroke of luck, every chance meeting, every conversation, bore fruit at that moment of my life.

First, there was the master class at La Roque d'Anthéron, in which I had wanted to take part because it was led by Jorge Bolet—the famous Jorge Bolet, a Cuban exiled in the United States after the revolution, a brilliant diplomat in his spare time, and a musician in his soul forever. I had seen pictures of him when he was just starting out. His Rudolph Valentino physique—he had been Dirk Bogarde's double in a film on the life of Franz Liszt—heralded an intensely seductive relationship with the world, with a touch of chic like the fruit atop the frosty triangles of glasses holding exotic cocktails: blue lagoons and green ti' punches. Jorge Bolet could play the entire repertoire, from Bach to Busoni, and Mussorgsky to Stravinsky, but he excelled mainly in playing pieces of pure virtuosity, on which his electric touch bestowed poetry and lyricism. He had the reputation of having revived Liszt, the Romantic repertoire in general, and Rachmaninoff in particular. He was seventy-three years old, and yet, reading about his sometimes extravagant life and listening to his recordings, I felt closer to him than to a great many of my peers. I wanted to come face-to-face with a master; I recognized him as such. And I could not work indefinitely by myself, off in my corner, without the approval or disapproval of an audience—whether a professor or the public.

I still remember my hairstyle on the day of the master class. My mother's hands pulled at my incredibly unruly mane, braiding my hair Roman-style before the concert, while I silently rehearsed the score in my mind. For Jorge Bolet, I had prepared a particularly difficult, one might even say athletic, piece: Franz Liszt's *Dante* Sonata. At the same time as I was mentally rehearsing, through the window of my room I gazed out at the hundred-year-old plane trees in the park, trees whose special smell always reminded me of Aix, autumn, and the start of classes. It was the sixth season for the festival that is known today as "the Mecca of the piano." This brief interlude, shared by pianists from around the world, felt somewhat like vacation; and yet at the same time it put you immediately in tune with excellence, with international competition. And what places to play! Silvacane Abbey and the Lake of the Alders—what better theaters for a Romantic concert? Now you try it: close your eyes and say these names, say them slowly, in a murmur . . . Silvacane Abbey, Lake of the Alders . . . Fairies and water sprites come to mind, don't they? Merlin and Melusina, under the magic wand of Orpheus.

At La Roque d'Anthéron, all you dream of is becoming one of the "greats" yourself one day, of someday being invited to give a concert, of inspiring the crowds—sweeping them away with you—in this temple made not of stone but of notes, built not in honor of the heroic violence of a battle or a barbarian dream but for the most delicate world there is, a long, caressing lullaby. Here, everything is geared toward excellence. The pianist has the choice from a half-dozen concert grand pianos. Imagine, if you are a car enthusiast, being in a garage filled with Ferraris, Jaguars, Maseratis, and Rolls-Royces. At La Roque, it is a succession of Steinways, Bösendorfers, Faziolis, Yamahas, and other legendary pianos—and prototypes, on top of it all—tuned by a star piano tuner, Denijs de Winter. Every evening, with these incredible instruments, the park shimmered with acoustic brilliance, and we plunged deep into music's very fiber.

The other magic thing about this place is that the greats stay on to listen to their peers, whether established stars or rising talent. No doubt you have heard what happened at Vlado Perlemuter's farewell concert?

"You were there, weren't you?" one is asked; at the memory, your correspondent's eyes begin to sparkle. For this last concert, you were of course in the audience. Like a nomad searching out the last drop of water in the desert, like the blackbird seeking the last cherry of spring, you go to harvest the final note played by this pianist of genius. All ears, barely breathing, weightless, to hear the notes, their echoes, and the silences that follow.

Vlado Perlemuter gives five encores—five unexpected, unhoped-for kisses—following his first farewell. The audience is in state of rapture. They leap from their seats, run to form a guard of honor on either side of the plane trees that line the walkway that the artist will take from the stage to the dressing rooms. That night, the waves of applause form a carriage for the great master of music.

That is La Roque d'Anthéron: a holy mass with a joyful and

reverent liturgy, intoned by a man with a passion for music. A few days at the festival there, and all doubts and uncertainties vanish.

"How are you going to understand what he says?" my mother said worriedly. "You don't speak English."

And Jorge Bolet didn't speak French. On the sign-up sheet for this master class, it was strongly recommended that students speak English. I paid no attention, convinced that my profound attraction for the repertoire that he had been playing for a half century augured a deep complicity between us, a reciprocal understanding that would break down the language barrier. I was not wrong. As soon as I saw him play, his powerful and sensual manner, I understood what he wanted to transmit to me. And as soon as I caught his eye, I knew that this incompatibility of language would be a minor detail. I played, and because we did not speak, we left each other with a smile in our eyes. I didn't know exactly what he thought of me, except that he seemed satisfied with my interpretation, and that was already incredible. I had come to receive an expert opinion in order to evaluate the quality of the work I had done so far.

"Hélène Grimaud? It's been a long, very long time since I encountered a talent of such extraordinary quality and sensibility of temperament."

Jorge Bolet confided this opinion to the journalist Alain Lompech in an interview published in *Le Monde.*

Everything took off from there. An article in a newspaper of record, the praise of a master of the piano, and a few hours later I received a visit from the man, who would become my agent, and from René Martin, the director of the festival.

An incredible feeling of joy stayed with me the entire afternoon following these visits and offers. I still remember those special hours. I had a feeling of physical exhaustion, as if I had finally arrived at a landing after slowly climbing a particularly steep flight of stairs. As if I had finally arrived at the terrace of the Tower of Victory in Chittaurgarh.

One of the most striking legends for me—and one in which the wolf, our hero, appears—is the story of the mandrake. What is a mandrake? An animal? A plant? It's rather something between the two, somewhere on the boundaries of the plant and animal kingdoms. If you try to pull it up, it cries out—a long, sad wail that enters the body like venom, spreading there in an intolerable pitch. In *Romeo and Juliet*, Juliet is terrified at the idea of its cry; it drives others mad.

Throughout history, it has intrigued naturalists, philosophers, and mathematicians. Pythagoras invented the term "anthropomorphous" for it, and the Roman agronomist Lucius Columella called it a "half-man." According to Pliny, the white mandrake is male, and the black is—of course—female. The odor of its leaves is so strong that most of those who smell it are rendered mute.

The roots have a human shape; hence, the long-standing superstition that the mandrake grows in abundance at the base of a gallows. In his *Pseudodoxia Epidemica*, published in 1646, Thomas Browne called this plant the "grease of hanged men." In 1913, the popular German novelist Hans Heinz Ewers referred to it as "semen."

In German, mandrake is called *Alraune*, which earlier was *Alruna*, both deriving from *rūn,* which means "mystery" or something hidden; *rūn* was later used to refer to the characters in the first Germanic alphabet (runes). Did the secret of the mandrake lie in the odor of its leaves? Absolutely, and for the ancient Greek physician Dioscorides, the plant was synonymous with the herb of Circe, the sorceress who wanted to cast a spell over wily Ulysses. What does Homer say about the mandrake? In Book X of *The Odyssey* we read: "The root was black, while the flower was as white as milk. Mortal men cannot uproot it, but the gods are all-powerful."

The gods? Only the gods? No, wolves as well. For Pliny, there were only two ways to harvest the mandrake. The first involves tracing three circles on the ground around it with a sword. Then you must look westward, holding your breath as long as possible: the smell of its leaves is so strong that ordinarily it can deprive men of the power of speech. The second way is to train a wolf to pull up the flower. Only the wolf is capable of doing so without causing endless misfortune. Above all, as it dies—none survive the ordeal—the wolf passes its power to the leaves of the mandrake. The passer of eternity, as it draws its final breath, the wolf makes them narcotic and magical.

According to, I think, the Qur'an, there are two types of people, those who suffer fate and those who choose to suffer it. I chose to suffer it and, take it all around; it has treated me favorably. That summer of 1987, there was the article in *Le Monde,* and the meeting with my agent and with René Martin, the director of the festival at La Roque d'Anthéron. Just before, I had been invited to give a recital at the festival of Aix-en-Provence, where Pierre Vozlinsky, the artistic director of the Orchestre de Paris, heard the broadcast live on the radio and asked me to meet Daniel Barenboim for an audition. And finally, the famous CD was released and, contrary to all my reservations, it was very well received and was awarded the Grand Prix du Disque. The producers at Denon asked me to record a second.

There was nothing very special or particular about all this, in fact—luck and its magic wand wrote the score; all I did was take the opportunities as they came along. First concerts, first recordings, first critical reviews in the press, first professional encounters. The musical path that I was on, beneath the green linden trees of the promenade, looked very straight and even incredible for a seventeen-year-old pianist.

I had no longing for my romantic relationship, just a slight suffering caused by the inevitable separation and the wounds that were inflicted. No regrets, rather a feeling of liberation. Should I be surprised? Should I suffer? I didn't miss love. Once obtained and conquered, it had oppressed more than satisfied me. Going it alone seemed much less discordant than being part of a couple. Thus, nothing sprang up along my path. But it's true that I was caught up in a musical movement, a departure, a pilgrimage.

Around me, girls my age talked about veils of tulle, of lace, of cradles and children—all projects that didn't interest me in the least. To tell the truth, I found them rather odd and slightly alarming. Love is no doubt the vision of the fire of things; for me, this vision was basically of another sort. Was it music? Yes, of course, but not only music. In the same way that I had always felt like an exile, elsewhere and not from here, I sensed that music would not entirely satisfy me. It was my equal; it was me in part; it was so strongly me that I did not need to focus on it. It didn't give me my goal in life. It was simultaneously the mystery and the answer to the mystery. It was not my goal but my companion, the mail coach that I boarded in my desire to cast off the mooring lines, so that I could, at last, extract from life the essence that I intuitively knew was there—the something that my entire being was reaching for and that I could not define, but which was the expectation, the delicious, thrilling expectation of a stranger that, I was certain, wanted nothing more than to reveal its name to me, its face, and its nature.

After these initial successes, people started to talk to me of a calling, of a career mapped out for me. For the first time I was thought of not as a simple student of the National Conservatory of Music, but as a musician, a pianist. And when in turn I looked at my life from this one point of view, a curious wind, a wild wind, worked its way through the cracks, blowing about and overturning everything.

The wolf is completely hot: it has a little of the characters of ethereal spirits and the manners of the lion. The ethereal spirits enjoy the company of its nature and accompany it. Thanks to its lion's nature, it knows and understands man and can smell him from afar. As soon as the wolf perceives a man, the ethereal spirits that accompany the wolf diminish that man's strength, because the man does not know, at that moment, that a wolf sees him. But when a man sees a wolf first, he has God in his heart and, by thinking of Him, causes the ethereal spirits as well as the wolf to flee.

If one suffers from gout, one should take equal amounts of blackcurrant and comfrey leaves; one crushes them in a mortar and then adds the fat of a wolf, in a slightly greater quantity. From this one makes a salve with which one rubs the painful areas. Then, on the second or third day, one enters a hot bath and evacuates the gout through perspiration. One must not remove the salve from one's skin before bathing, because it is so powerful that the gout can in no way remain where the salve has been spread.

If someone, because of illnesses that have seized his head, flies into a fit, you must shave his head, then cook a wolf in water, after having removed the skin and entrails. Then wash the head of the raging one with the cooking water, after having blocked his eyes, ears, and mouth with cloths so that the water does not enter: because if this liquid enters his body, his madness will increase as if it were poison. Repeat this for three days—even if the madness is strong, he will return to his senses. If he does not stand for having his eyes, nose, and mouth blocked, you must then soak a cloth in the cooking liquid and wrap his head with the still-warm cloth, and leave it on his head for about an hour. Repeat this for three days and the man will return to his proper senses. When he is better, wash the head with hot wine to remove the fat.

It was Saint Hildegard of Bingen who wrote this, in *The Book of Subtleties of the Diverse Nature of Things*, sometime between 1105, the year when she was entrusted to the care of the Benedictines (she was eight years old), and September 17, 1179, when she died in the convent at Rupertsberg, Germany, that she had founded.

Hildegard had visions; moreover, she wrote them down. Very early, she had one of the Garden of Eden: she wanted to tear away the veil that the Fall had placed between our souls and Paradise. Eden is not situated in the beyond; it is here, here and now, to the extent that each of us knows how to reestablish the original harmony between nature and human beings. And above all, to the extent that we want to. And here she is reconciling mind and body, body and soul, to create metamorphoses. She was a brilliant and inspired woman who spoke of the griffon and the whale, of the spirit of the linden tree and the flight of the chaffinch. She wrote her recipes for the spirit and for medicine. At the same time, she sang and composed oratorios—it was said that she had a marvelous voice—in a twelfth century that was so rough, so filled with the terror of being alive. Hildegard of Bingen, with her music, sang the fertility of the world and the soul.

She composed music that was truly angelic, she sang, and she drew from nature the ingredients for her recipes: she was enchanting. Claude Mettra, in his foreword to *The Book of Subtleties of the Diverse Nature of Things,* rightly notes the extent to which this book inspired Ingmar Bergman's *Hour of the Wolf.*

Hour of the wolf? "One of those special moments when, over and above the cares and borders of everyday life, a strange trembling runs through the human heart, like the call of an unknown world, of which we are both its children and its outcasts. A painful revelation for our fragile souls, one which generally serves only to nourish melancholy mirages in us. Hildegard is one who wanted to see that which lay beyond premonition, at the heart of revelation."

For all of these reasons, I love this female figurehead, leaning out in front of the others, fearless, dominating and penetrating the unknown. And this strange trembling that ran through her heart, I knew it in my turn. It had the force of the wind.

Music, nature, wolves, everything is there.

In addition, the wind was blowing more and more frequently, this wind of chaos and tempest. This desert wind that swirled in coarse farandoles, in fantastic sarabandes, a wind for which the nomads have no name. How could they give a name to something that obeys neither the sand, the scorching sun, nor even the points of the compass? This wind had kindled my rebellious spirit when people gave me advice that did not resonate inside me. I had taken the famous audition with Daniel Barenboim, as agreed, and the conductor of the Orchestre de Paris had offered an engagement for the following season after hearing me play Liszt's *Dante* Sonata. But although he tried to teach me, in his open, friendly manner, particularly about the symphonic repertoire of which I knew practically nothing—inviting me to sit in on rehearsals—we once came into conflict regarding method. Thus, I couldn't understand why he asked me to stay and work the evening before my concert at the Théâtre de la Ville, when the pianist Martha Argerich and the violinist Gidon Kremer were playing on the same evening. I would certainly learn more listening to them than by doggedly sitting at the keyboard another three hours. And so I went to applaud them.

Daniel thought I was stubborn and difficult, and my agent shared his opinion. I gave him a hard time as well: I refused to show up for an appointment that he had set up with a famous foreign conductor to audition me—his way of conducting put me off. I refused to play Saint-Saëns's Second Concerto: it didn't please me.

Events smiled on me, and yet, around me, there was a sort of negative vibration, an element that thwarted my relationship to others and to the world. I really had the impression that everything was becoming more and more difficult, as in a nightmare when you try to walk but your feet are fastened to the ground, when every movement becomes laborious and exhausting. Even my looks did me disservice. A thousand times, among the questions people would ask, there would be the inevitable, "You're kind of pretty— why don't you try to do something else?" Paris would have perhaps preferred me to be a young model on the fashion runway, or a nice student eating popcorn with her boyfriend at the movies. Paris refused to open its arms to me. I still can't say if I was suffering from a sort of image problem. It worried me, to be sure. People's attitudes toward me, on the other hand, set me on edge. "Too beautiful to be intelligent," for example. Or, "With looks like hers, she doesn't need to work." Or, "How many hours a day did you say you practiced?" and I understood that the person asking was converting those hours into a huge loss, pure waste compared with the frivolous life that my blond hair and blue eyes would have made possible.

In fact, the pain of this profession is not in the ardent work at the keyboard—which is sometimes a total loss, since not everyone makes it—but rather in the way others perceive you. There are people who cannot cross the holy barrier that they have erected between themselves and you and the music—and it's a bit frightening to find yourself on a pedestal. There are the ones who wait. To talk to you, to meet you, to touch you. Those are called fans; they give you a great deal, but they demand a response that is commensurate with their love.

I recognize them in the concert hall, and I talk with them if I can. Every person is unique, in my mind. But they want more. They want a personal connection—a friendship. This is unthinkable. It's impossible to have a relationship with tens of thousands of people. How can I explain to them that I gave them everything onstage during the concert? Up there, I truly played for each one of them, and not for a mass of people called the public.

I will never forget the Englishman who showed up at my door in the United States with a backpack and his girlfriend.

"We'd like to visit with you . . ."

Certainly. I was moved: after all, they had crossed the Atlantic to fulfill this dream. But I was in a business meeting with a manager from my record company.

"You should have let me know you were hoping to come visit. In any case, I'm sorry, but I can't invite you in."

With no further ado, I shut the door on them. They were furious. A few days later, I received an insulting letter . . . and a few months after that, an apology.

But I wasn't there yet; it was the last few years of the 1980s. I was still feeling my way along, even though, thanks to my agent, I had started to give concerts abroad: in Germany, a pleasant surprise; in Switzerland, under the direction of Eliahu Inbal; and then the New American Chamber Orchestra engaged me for a tour in Japan—Tokyo and Osaka; and then London.

I discovered my first trips and the very particular world of airports—and at first, I loved flying. I learned about the nights alone in the hotel after the concert and the difficulty of going to sleep, my head haunted by the music, playing and replaying the film of my performance, every neuron alert and firing. Some concerts were good; others were, frankly, bad. I was uneven, without experience, and lacking a definitive vision of the works.

Leon Fleisher had been right to recommend patience and silence until I had found my path, my sound.

Happily, at that time, there was the festival of Lockenhaus and the decisive meetings that took place there. Martha Argerich, first and foremost. Martha the Lion.

Martha is the force that dominates everything in its path, the sovereignty of vital energy. She feels events from the inside, in their entirety. A woman of air. With her, things were not transmitted in words, but in the silence they inhabited: there was no need to talk, or very little. What was essential was expressed anyway by a way of being.

She played with Gidon Kremer, and the two of them were at the peak of what they could create together; they personified the miracle of sharing. Then there was the place, the philosophy of that place that brought young musicians into contact with more experienced artists, and had them play together. Consequently, spontaneity and invention played a large role in the three or four concerts that were scheduled each day.

Every morning, an organizer would pass among us, asking, "What would you like to play today?"

Groups formed. We decided on a piece. We rehearsed a bit. Naturally, quartets and quintets were prepared two or three days in advance.

"Before working on a piece, an intellectual preparation is both necessary and indispensable. Everything must be taken apart and then reconstructed, everything fused together."

Gidon Kremer explained how to approach a work, how to find its unique sound by analyzing all of the opportunities, by exploring all of the possibilities. "Why not like this?" was the first, the primordial, question to ask.

Starting with this festival, I diligently followed Gidon's advice. I applied his recommendations to the letter, even at the risk of instrumental paralysis. I asked myself so many questions that I could no longer separate myself from the score or get enough perspective to actually lay hands on the piano. Some days I thought I understood. I had a fleeting glimpse of what could be and would be—I knew that was it, exactly like that—but between those brief glimmers, those rare moments of illumination, I groped my way along in the dark. I struggled in the void to resolve difficulties, and sometimes weeks passed without my finding the solution. Speed was a particularly difficult problem for me. I couldn't keep myself from playing as fast as possible. I had the impression that the keys of the piano went down too quickly, as if the piano had a life of its own and was casting a spell on my hands, dragging them along in a mad dash, a crescendo. It was horribly disagreeable, and sometimes I had to stop working altogether to break this habit.

I made mistakes and I called those errors by their real name: failures. My failures allowed me to make progress. In this profession, everything is a mind game: if you don't have enough confidence in yourself, you will never reach your potential, but if you never fail, you will never progress.

Often I thought I was saved, and then, once again, I would be tormented by doubt. I advanced like a mountaineer across a snow bridge between two glaciers, my every step hesitant, testing the safety of the snow, evaluating the risk of an avalanche, eliminating the risky paths that led to dead ends, and even to death. I crept forward on eggshells. And sometimes I wavered.

I corrected my tendencies to first throw myself completely into an interpretation and then a second later, without having made the necessary connection, to want to destroy what I had begun. At the same time, I learned that perfection is not to be sought at any price. It doesn't exist—it is the best way to lose one's way and one's crucially important point of view. I thought about this perfection, and I understood that it meant giving everything that I had, in my own way, without betraying myself in order to do what I thought would please this or that person or the audience. This discovery strengthened my love for the Romantic repertoire; it is already so excessive, so subjective, that there's no need to overinterpret the sensitivity of its composers. The only way to be poignant is to be direct.

Gidon Kremer taught me how to analyze a score, and from Martha Argerich I learned the vital force of intuition. What exactly did she give me? Not any one piano technique, but rather, and much more important, the confirmation that I had to become what I was, as she had become the person she was. She taught me that I must face the inevitable: the inevitable in ourselves that, after all, is the only thing that can save us.

"When one asks children what they want to be when they grow up, they never say 'a critic,' which proves that it's a job for losers." It's impossible not to laugh with François Truffaut, who was a critic himself early on, at this statement that he put into the mouth of one of his characters.

Shall I give you an example? Who are these lines about? "Never before have we been so complacent in the face of the hideous. Is it lucidity? No, sadism. The author wallows in the stench of it. The heart tightens. The skin crawls. And one is rigid with embarrassment, the embarrassment of being there. Yes, I lowered my head, I didn't dare look at the stage anymore. I had the feeling that I was taking part in an obscene vision." This author who "wallows in the stench of it"—according to the sage judgment of this oracle who today is completely forgotten—is none other than Samuel Beckett, and the play, perhaps his most beautiful, was *Happy Days*. A nice job, criticism, which too often consists of finding the worst in the best, and vice versa, for lack of a personal or objective point of view.

All joking aside, no one can deny the discerning heights that criticism can attain when it is the work of musicians like Debussy and Boulez, authors like Borges and Blanchot or, simply, beings who are still capable of being moved. In such cases, criticism is a parallel art, an homage paid by artists to their peers, attempting to transpose an emotion using other means, that of reason and of the mind. Baudelaire wrote about Wagner: "All great poets become naturally, inevitably, critics."

Unfortunately, the reverse is rarely true. And I'm sorry, but these individuals lack the critical experience of stage fright, the face-to-face encounter with a hall in which every person is different from every other, where every listener (among them the critic) expects from you a distinct emotion, a specific response to his or her point of view about the work. They are missing the one-on-one encounter with themselves, seated at a piano whose keys suddenly resemble gleaming, formidable fangs. Face to face with doubt, despite hours of research and practice.

One of these critics, at one point well known, writing for a conservative French newspaper, at the beginning of my career called me a little goat with no taste, good only for jumping about onstage. A few years later, he wrote that, contrary to his expectations, I hadn't changed a bit: I was still that pianist who deserved to be whipped, a booming Valkyrie! Still later, he admitted in the pages of the same paper that he had been moved by one of my concerts that he had attended; he was thrilled to have the chance once again to publicly change his opinion about me. That was the last one.

Today, I take the decrees of the press in stride. The public doesn't need someone to prescribe whom they should like or not—they are adults, passionate and demanding, and it is for them that I play. But initially, during the first concerts in Paris, it was a nightmare. I needed to have the encouragement of masters such as Pierre Barbizet, Jorge Bolet, Daniel Barenboim, and Leon Fleisher so as to not be affected by such contradictory statements.

I admit that, in the beginning, these contradictions tormented me, until the day I took a good, hard look at them and discovered that, basically, there were more good reviews than bad. What struck me to the heart was how excessively cruel the bad ones were, their desire to go in for the kill. I considered them to be worthless, completely sterile, inasmuch as I was able to keep the upper hand, not over the others, but over my own uncertainties. An artist's primary critic is herself: her goal is not illusory perfection, which would be stillborn—no one can speak exactly for the composers, or for their desires. What all real artists aim for is to use their lives to animate the life of the work they are playing, to give their entire being to it, in that perfect abandon—which is love.

The great painters never tried to reproduce the reality of faces line for line; they started from a model in order to draw from it the deepest part of existence. And then, what is there to *reproduce* in music? There is no model of the ideal interpretation, drawn up like the blueprint of a perfect temple, like a living human being. There is and can only be an encounter with the existence of music that is played. "Somewhere in the unfinished."

❧

After the Lockenhaus festival, I fell ill. An infectious mononucleosis brought me back home, back to Aix. My body was very weak, and strangely, my thoughts were much sharper, more agile.

I gave myself up to the care of my parents, to my father's tender vigilance and my mother's cheerfulness—then I returned to Paris, where Daniel Barenboim had given up waiting for me: the message I had left for him about my illness and the length of my convalescence never reached him. He thought I was somewhat unpredictable, and therefore was not overly surprised that I had disappeared without a word.

Destiny is often fed by incidents of this sort, these little glitches in time, misunderstandings and mixups. This one plunged me into a solitude that was both useful and much-needed. Barenboim wasn't waiting for me anymore? It was at this moment that I decided to withdraw from the world. I no longer wanted to be seen.

I moved into Gidon Kremer's place, with whom I had started a precious friendship. He had loaned me his apartment whenever he was away on tours that kept him far from Paris. Sometimes I slipped off to Switzerland to visit Martha Argerich, who, with insane generosity, kept an assembly of young musicians around her. I didn't work anymore, except on scores. I spent my time reading endlessly, books and many notes. Focused on the strength of my inertia, I refused to leave the apartment. From the window, like a bird, I contemplated with supreme detachment the hustle and bustle of Montparnasse beneath me. They were over, those delicious wanderings of my early days in Paris, when I surrendered myself to the flow of bodies in the torrent of the streets, devouring the faces that fascinated me. I stewed, I ruminated, I despaired, weighed down by a jumble of characters in novels and too few acquaintances. I didn't want to see anyone. I didn't even know how to write the word "joy" anymore.

As a child, I had wanted to grow up because I imagined age as an obstacle to flight and childhood as a purgatory. But contrary to what I had thought, now that I was living my own life, nothing had improved, nothing was better than I had thought. I was free, completely free, and yet I was as bad off as could be—I could barely keep my head above water. I had never experienced such an intense feeling of being cut off from the world, from beauty, and from pleasure. I had the fleeting sensation of being dissociated from a whole.

During those interminable days, I remember finding in a book of aphorisms this sentence by Léon Bloy: "When you meet a great person, ask first where his suffering is." At that point in my existence, I could define mine. I was tormented by a feeling of powerlessness, and worse, of being useless. My suffering was an action, and the contemplation of that suffering was an abyss. A huge black hole dug itself into my chest. It communicated not with infinite space or the cosmos or the dizzying architecture of music, but instead—like a hole in the bottom of a boat—with the murky waters of the ocean depths, swallowing even the shadows there.

I was experiencing something like an acute loss of self. The abandonment of the self by the self, after being completely forsaken. At the festival in La Roque d'Anthéron in 1989, where I had been invited for the third time, I was in a deep depression. I really thought I would never come out of it. I was disenchanted with the world and with the people I met. Before the lane that was lined with the plane trees that had enchanted me, murmuring with the mistral and with summer's perfume, despite the memory of my mother's laughter and her hands plaiting my hair, despite the memory of that something I was still waiting for—something that, without my being able to lay hold of it, had already disappeared with a sigh—and despite my youth and its strength, I had—for the first and last time in my life—the wild, sudden, and uncontrollable desire to disappear.

One day, during a telephone call, a friend told me, "We can be essential only when we are suffering. It encourages us to remain honest."

The mating season for wolves begins in late winter, from February until early March. It is often the lead female, the bolder of the two, that signifies to the male her readiness. Her preference is for the top-ranking male in the pack hierarchy. Nevertheless, the other young wolves can seek to win her.

Once the couple forms, the female will usually remain faithful to her companion her entire life, and vice versa. During the gestation period, the female prepares a cozy den, which she lines with dried grasses and tufts of hair for the litter to come, some sixty-three days after mating. The she-wolf never has to fear—as is the case with members of the cat family—that the male will eat her young.

On average, litters consist of between one and eight little wolves, though sometimes there can be ten or eleven. They are born blind and motionless. The mortality rate is high: up to fifty and even sixty percent.

The she-wolf's milk is very nourishing and gives the pups a

good chance of surviving to the age of eight weeks, at which point they are weaned and fed on meat regurgitated by either parent. As long as the pups are incapable of leaving the area of the den, some other member of the pack watches over them while the rest of the pack hunt. A mother wolf is one of the most attentive teachers in the animal world. Her maternal instinct stems from the hormone prolactin, which is plentiful in the wolf's system. When the pups are three to four months old, she begins to bring live prey back to the den in order to toughen and teach her young. When the dominant alpha couple returns from the hunt, the pups rush over to them, biting and licking the underside of their muzzles, which stimulates the regurgitation reflex. This behavior, which continues into adulthood, shows submission and even affection. Sometimes they are part of a ritual of thanks, and indicate the respect that one individual wants to show to another.

The she-wolf's fertility and maternal instinct are the basis of legends, and without doubt one of the most famous legends in antiquity: The wicked King Amulius threw two children into the swamp to die, devoured by snakes and vermin. These twins, Romulus and Remus, were discovered by a she-wolf, which took them to her lair and suckled them, thus saving them from certain death. As an adult, Romulus founded the city of Rome, and the she-wolf thus became the emblem of the city to which she guaranteed the immortality of an empire.

Historians have endlessly analyzed the origins of this myth, positing, for example, that the brothels of Rome were called *lupanaria*—"places of she-wolves"—because prostitutes were called *lupae*, "she-wolves" in Latin, and that from there, it's just a step to the idea that Romulus and Remus were in fact saved and suckled by a kindhearted streetwalker with a large bosom.

For all that, the Romans did not joke about their founding myth. Every sign and incident involving a wolf was scrupulously recounted and confided to the augurs for interpretation. Thus, in the late autumn of the year 401, news of a barbarian invasion spread a wave of terror throughout the Italian peninsula. This frightful prospect was reinforced by the appearance of a comet and several lunar eclipses.

"But," as the poet Claudian wrote in his *De Bello Getico*, "what terrified men's minds still more was the portent of the two slaughtered wolves. Before the emperor's face as he practiced his cavalry upon the plain two wolves savagely attacked his escort. Slain by darts they disclosed a horrid portent and a wondrous sign of what was to be. In each animal, on its being cut open, was found a human hand, in the stomach of one a left hand, in that of the other a right was discovered, both still twitching, the fingers stretched out and suffused with living blood. Wouldst thou search out the truth, the beast as messenger of Mars foretold that the foe would fall before the emperor's eyes. As the hands were found to be living when the stomachs were cut open, so, when the Alps had been broken through, the might of Rome was to be discovered unimpaired. But fear, ever a poor interpreter, read disaster in the portent; severed hands, it was said, and a nursing wolf threatened destruction on Rome and her empire!"

This text was read by Claudian in 402 in the temple of Apollo, the wolf-god. No one seemed astonished by this story, or by the fateful, bloody hands that foretold destiny. These wolves were called the "wolves of Milan," after the place where the Emperor Honorius, to whom they appeared, was exercising his troops. For a long time, this historic episode was the subject of much talk, and it was relegated to a status of myth or legend. A wolf stuffed with intact human arms, indicating to the prince—like an air traffic controller telling an airplane pilot—the right way to bring the crew back safe and sound? The fact remains that, a few years later, Alaric and his Goths, with the support of Radagaisus, entered Italy and were defeated.

There is another legend that has aroused a great deal of doubt: the one about the wolf of Gubbio, tamed by a laying on of hands and the sign of the cross by Francis of Assisi. "Brother Wolf, in the name of Christ . . ." And Brother Wolf obeyed. The inhabitants of Gubbio were astonished by this miracle, and as a sign of gratitude and friendship, they promised the wolf that they would feed and care for him. Thus, peacefully, petted by children, spoiled by the womenfolk, the wolf of Gubbio watched over the town. Pure legend? Historians maintain that this wolf was simply the name that the inhabitants of the town had given to a fierce bandit who was terrorizing and robbing them. Unless, of course, it referred to the feudal lord of the region, who was merciless with his flock. These explanations were accepted until 1873, when, during the restoration of a chapel devoted to Saint Francis that had been built during his lifetime, the skull and remains of an enormous wolf were discovered beneath a flagstone.

What did these two years of independence teach me in particular? Certain things about the nature of music, which was also my nature. I was a free, uninhibited human being, not born for nests or for groups. Above all, I wanted to advance according to my instincts and desires, to continue to follow my path without the fear that one day it would be lost in quicksand. Those two years taught me that solitude is the essential place where I can be myself, with myself; it is there that reality takes shape under the sign of desire—only that which one desires from oneself for oneself tends to be real.

I understood that I am closer to outcry than silence—I often protest, and I will always do so. In addition, my relationship to silence is more fantasy than reality. And yet I can go a long time without speaking, when the spoken word seems superfluous to me. Sometimes I practice a silent asceticism, until I hear in the silence the music of silence itself—a nothingness, but a nothingness that speaks and listens. Music is an extension of silence, which precedes it, and which resounds at the heart of a piece. It is the door to an Elsewhere of speech, that which speech cannot say—and which silence can say, by quieting it. Music without silence? I call that noise. On the other hand, I'm sorry to admit, I am not wise enough to keep silent, even if I know its value.

"All pleasure seeks eternity—a deep and profound eternity," wrote Nietzsche.

Why does this phrase always remind me of the story of Fanny Hensel, born Mendelssohn? And that of the young woman from the turn of the century (I am speaking about the early 1900s), who was seized by a writing frenzy, a necessity that woke her in the night, forced her to leave the marriage bed, and plunged her into a feverish joy that took her away from others, her family, children, and friends, and especially her husband. This young American woman, whose name escapes me, ended by accepting and even demanding—since she was persuaded of her immense madness by her husband—that she be placed in a psychiatric hospital; and submitted to other, much harsher treatments, because her desire and her pleasure, which she fulfilled by filling page after page with novels and poems, did not disappear. One day something inside her vanished. The cure was too severe, the electroshock sessions too frequent. Although he was momentarily distraught, her husband did not file suit against her doctors or ask for an explanation. He and his family had gotten what they wanted: his wife, her gaze unfixed, remained seated the whole day long on a day bed, absorbed in making pretty lacework. Her permanent, vague smile wafted over her furniture, her servants, her children, without anyone really knowing what made her float like that, what vision, what briefly glimpsed eternity. But sometimes, without her smile ever leaving her pretty lips—at a time when publishers and critics were finally reading the pages and pages that she had bound herself, pages covered in her fine handwriting—her hand grew weak. The blue vein that beat at her wrist accelerated its rhythm. The needle, the lacemaking cushion, and the multicolored silk threads slipped to the floor; then, imperceptibly, her fingers traced in the air the outline of a movement that seemed to be that of writing, a phrase perhaps, a word, a world that was henceforth lost forever.

This story, which could be called "A Woman and Creation," has occurred many times in many forms. Another example is Fanny Zippora Mendelssohn, the eldest of four children, including Felix, her brother, who was four years younger. Fanny received a solid education, and very early on displayed prodigious musical gifts. At thirteen, she gave an astonishing interpretation of *The Well-Tempered Clavier* by Johann Sebastian Bach; Goethe noted admiringly that she "played like a man." The comparison was meant to be highly complimentary, of course.

Then Fanny began to create—interpretation was not enough. She rushed off to concerts, she played, she composed. She loved only music. She announced to her family that this would be her life, because it was her calling, her wish.

"Music will perhaps become Felix's profession, whilst for you it can and must only be an ornament, never the reason for your being and your activity," her father said.

By his veto, her father, Abraham Mendelssohn, let her know his opinion on the matter and moreover, the opinion of his century, society, and world. Fanny was fifteen years old; she was unhappy, but she obeyed. She was a woman; her father had money; she would thus be a bourgeois woman: that is, wife, mother, and keeper of the house. The only concession to her free spirit was her marriage to Wilhelm Hensel, who was an artist, a famous one: he was the official court painter to the King of Prussia.

For all that, Fanny continued to compose "for the drawer," while watching over the upbringing of her one child—a son—as it should be.

"There truly exists a music that is as if one had extracted music's quintessence, as if it were the very soul of music: such are your melodies. Oh Jesus! I know none better."

Felix, her brother, heard these works that had been written in secret. He published a collection of them, under his own name, admittedly. It was a resounding success. Fanny saw encouragement in this. During her Sunday-morning concerts, she dared to play her own repertoire. Clara and Robert Schumann, Franz Liszt, Niccolò Paganini and Bettina von Arnim came to lend their applause. Fanny became more daring: in 1834, she offered her "Ave Maria" to an English publisher, who accepted it. She was exhilarated: "I have no wish to deny the joy that the publication of my music brings to me, nor how much it contributes to increasing my good humor. It is a very heady feeling to know such success only at an age when success normally ends for women, if ever they had known it." There came an exhilarated outpouring of cantatas, lieder, and songs.

Her father died. Her brother inherited his firm and intractable opposition to any sort of musical fame for Fanny. Depressed for a time, she gave in. She returned to creating clandestinely for eleven years. But one morning: "Although I know that, in truth, this is against the wishes of Felix, I have now decided to publish my things. The publishers Bote and Bock have made me offers that an amateur has perhaps never before received, and Schlesinger's offers are even more dazzling. I don't imagine in the slightest that this will continue, but for the moment I am happy that my best pieces will be published since I have now made the decision."

Fatigue, sadness, and depression returned—for having saddened her brother, the famous Felix Mendelssohn, who was receiving acclaim in Berlin?

"I am in the midst of a distressing period, I am unsuccessful at anything musical, and I have not written a single measure since my trio."

On May 14, 1847—she was forty-one years old—Fanny died suddenly, in a heartbeat, during the rehearsal of the latest work published by her brother, *Walpurgisnacht.*

One day the telephone rang.

It had been silent for so long, in the Montparnasse apartment, that the ringing itself seemed rusted. It yanked me out of my torpor, and the reading of a book that I had been slogging through, my thoughts pulled along line after line by a plot whose beginning I had already forgotten. It was raining in Paris. The Montparnasse Tower was dripping wet. I hesitated. Was it my mother? Gidon? Martha? "If at ten rings, whoever it is doesn't hang up, then . . ."

At twelve, I picked up the receiver.

It was none of the above; it was my patient and faithful agent. In a somewhat weary voice, he said: "Hélène? I was just about to hang up."

And then, straight to business: "I have a trip to help you take your mind off things. A tour in the United States. Here's the situation: an agent for Columbia Artists, Greg Gleasner, heard one of your records. He wants to represent you over there."

The United States? On your mark, get set, go! I jumped at the chance, eager to put an ocean between my old and new selves. I was thrilled.

"Your first concert will be in Cleveland."

I had no idea where Cleveland was, in which state, on what coast. I would have gone to Little Rock or Minimum City if I could have. In addition, it wasn't the plane that took off for Cleveland, but me. Other than playing with the wonderful Cleveland Orchestra, nothing really noteworthy happened there, except my clear and determined decision to return to the United States. Cleveland! The name rang like the clarion call of the Light Brigade coming to my rescue. Adieu, Paris! Adieu, inertia and doubt!

Looking straight into Greg Gleasner's eyes, I said: "I would come back here anytime to play more concerts. I loved the experience, really."

"You don't speak English."

No, but I spoke music fluently, my beautiful language, my universal tongue. I assured him that this was only a temporary stumbling block. I promised that I would be bilingual for my next trip. He told me that he was going to look into it and think about it. The welcome had been warm in Cleveland, so why not?

I decided not to sign up for any sort of official course, rather to employ a completely personal method for learning English. I would listen and understand.

Suspended in this waiting period, my body was present in Paris but my mind was already wandering far away. In the images coming from the television, the VCR, and the movie screens. From morning to night, I went from one film to the next, and always in

English. I took in ready-made expressions that I learned by heart. I went from a love story to a Vietnam war film to a historical epic to a western, as long as they were in English. I rented dozens of videocassettes from the rental store on my street, while wolfing down ham sandwiches.

I assumed that I had to speak English to work in the United States. And I had to be convincing in what I said, assured in my pronunciation when I answered their "Why Brahms?" or "And Schumann?"

Six months later, Greg Gleasner called me back; we spoke in English from start to finish. We agreed on a three-week tour. The concerts would start in Washington, D.C., and end in Florida.

The end of the trip in Florida, and then back to Paris?

It was out of the question; that mustn't happen.

And it didn't.

Eight

I couldn't say at what moment, on what day, or at what hour of that American tour I knew that I would never return to live in France. The idea came to me gradually, perhaps because in city after city, from concert hall to interview, I felt like I was a musician, a respected, professional pianist. I had the feeling of being accepted, far from gossip and questions, protected from a reputation that had sprung up without my knowing it after I had deserted the Conservatory.

In the United States, I was no longer out of step. No one found me strange. The question was whether I played well, whether I was good and musically compelling. Nobody cared about the rest. Since they have no traditions (even though they have a particular way of life), Americans are not snobbish. And, paradoxically, although they are capable of marveling at everything, they are never astonished.

Here, I sensed an impressive energy, a strong forward motion. I guessed right away that anyone who wanted to accomplish something here had a chance to succeed. On top of that, I was immediately moved by the warmth of the welcome I received. I had always found it difficult to get along with people, but in this country the approach was easy and extremely simple; no one ever imposed himself or herself.

The tour that Greg Gleasner had put together ended in Florida, and that is where I met Jeff, a bassoon player. He invited me to return. It was at the exact moment he extended the invitation that my desire to stay surfaced, like the first, enormous breath of air filling one's lungs after a very deep dive.

In the time it took to slide the key under the door in Paris, throw my two pairs of jeans and toiletries into a suitcase, along with a few books for sustenance, I became a citizen of Tallahassee, the capital of Florida and a completely boring city, stuck right in the middle of nowhere, in a flat and densely wooded countryside.

Of course, Florida always evokes images of heavenly coastlines and eternal sunshine; everglades teeming with all sorts of scales—sharp-toothed alligators and lazy fish—and the swish of pink flamingo wings. None of this applied to Tallahassee. It is a little ways from the ocean, away from the magic water sources; there's no gentle lapping or powerful backwash, no music with the scent of salt or hazelnut trees by the river. The city's EKG was absolutely flat, despite the excellence of its university, which has at its center a very complete music department.

To be honest, I didn't like Florida, and much later, I wondered if I had entered into this relationship merely in order to settle in the United States. But I had boarded the train of destiny, and I was determined not to get off. I had chosen to be in Tallahassee, at the end of the earth, completely aware that I was in the last turn before the homestretch. I knew that I was on the threshold of something inexorable. My backpack was filled with inexhaustible reserves of patience. I felt at peace.

Jeff traveled a great deal. I left often for Europe, where I gave a large number of my concerts, mostly in Germany, and my affection for that country and its music-loving audiences never ceased to grow. I continued to work on my scores, to work out my discoveries on the piano. I read, and I went out for many walks accompanied by Jeff's only dog, Harvey, a German shepherd-husky mix. Her presence and her frolicking around me made me happy—it was as if Ripp, my great-grandfather's dog, and Rock, my neighbors' pointer, were finally mine and mine alone.

Often on these walks I got caught up in how exotic the place was: the fantastic enormity of a pecan tree entangled in creepers, or the strange call of a bird, and even, one day, at the edge of the city, a slow, prehistoric, solemn tortoise reminded me just how far I was from Paris. I remembered my recurring dream and I shuddered.

After the third or fourth walk, my presence in the neighborhood was noticed. My neighbors surprised me with a little visit and a welcome party.

In a few minutes, a table was set up in the yard and coolers revealed six-packs of cold beer and Dr Pepper. There were homemade cakes, popcorn, and everything needed to make sandwiches. In an instant, a stack of white bread spread with tuna, mayonnaise, lettuce, and cold chicken towered to the sky. The conversation rumbled along like the humming of bees, powerful and nonstop. I was a bit tired. It was hot. From time to time in the wide, quiet street, a huge Chrysler bounced over the speed bumps that allowed the neighborhood children to safely cross the street while chasing balls.

"You often go walking to the north of the neighborhood, isn't that right?"

A man of about forty, king-size beer in hand, smiled at me. I agreed. In that area, there were fewer houses, and the abundant undergrowth allowed Harvey to run where she wanted and hunt to her heart's content.

"Listen . . ."

The guests drew close around me, with their beautiful teeth, beautiful hair, and big smiles ("Hi! Where are you from?"). I understood in a flash that they had discussed what they were going to tell me.

"Watch yourself. There's a man up there, a Vietnam vet. He's not right in the head. Definitely crazy. We think he's dangerous."

All at once, everyone began talking about this subject. The sinister individual had weapons, an arsenal. Yes, in the United States it was perfectly possible. A misanthrope who went out only at night. He kept strange animals at his place, snakes for sure, or poisonous spiders, real dangerous ones, no doubt about that. So did I promise to be careful? Intrigued, I promised.

For several days, the story of this stranger kept running through my mind. Did Jeff know him? No, but like everyone else, he had just heard about him.

"It doesn't make any sense to go wandering around up there or taking any risks," he added in the same breath.

Of course, the area north of the neighborhood became the place where I took all my walks. I wasn't afraid; I was curious. Besides, I have always liked situations that remind me of just how deliciously dangerous life is. And I had Harvey by my side, didn't I? She was good at discouraging unwanted company, my affectionate bodyguard.

But after a concert tour and my return to the house, the mystery of the "cobra man," as I had baptized him, completely left my mind.

The wolf was dreaded, but also venerated for its medicinal qualities. Like certain tribes who devoured their enemies' livers in order to appropriate their courage, our ancestors prepared many remedies in which the wolf was the principal ingredient. In old collections of recipes and arcane volumes of spells, those afflicted with chronic colic were instructed to grill the ears of a wolf and soak them in a broth made from bats. Before eating them, it was advised, one should steep them and then drink the liquid very hot.

For epilepsy, a dried wolf's eye hung around the sufferer's neck worked wonders. A mounted wolf's tooth attached to a baby's bib protected the child against accidents. The wolf's liver, dried in the oven, relieved hepatic diseases if eaten and warts if applied as a poultice. Rubbing a wolf's claw gently on an infant's gums would help its teeth to grow and be strong. Dried wolf's tongue, worn in the same manner as the eye, warded off gossips and rumormongers. As a bonus, it ensured winnings at gambling.

In addition to working like a charm against certain illnesses, the wolf was also effective against evil spells and for attracting good influences—a wolf skin, worn as a collar or a tie, made one lucky in love. Made into breeches, it gave young soldiers courage and pugnacity in battle.

The wolf's muzzle, dried and ground into powder, kept away demons and misfortune, while the tail, buried in the barnyard of a farm, kept away evil vibrations and protected the animals.

The wolf's bite, if it did not carry rabies, cured swelling and every type of tumor.

Thus, one needed wolves, and they had to be killed.

Medicine was not the only pretext for capturing wolves. Protecting herds and game, as well as the pure thrill of the hunt gave additional reasons to hunt them down, to the point of planning, throughout Europe, the total destruction of the species. In the fifteenth century, England demanded that these beasts disappear: any region that did not furnish its quota of cadavers (three hundred wolves a year for Wales alone) was very heavily taxed. It was the same in Germany and Poland, but the wolves that were massacred were replaced by new hordes coming from Russia. For centuries, wolves were killed, tortured, cut up, skinned, poisoned, and trapped at an incredible rate: some 1,100 wolves were destroyed in France in 1884 alone.

To keep up this systematic slaughter, hunting parties were organized and bonuses awarded to the killers. Killing a pregnant wolf was particularly well rewarded, and its pelt brought a good price on the market. Were peasants letting the enemy get away too often? Charlemagne invented the Louvetiers ("Wolf Hunters"). This corps was made official by François I, and it was revived by Napoleon. This special army waged permanent war against "the red and black beasts"—mostly wolves, but also foxes, badgers, boars, and wildcats. But hunting wolves remained the favorite sport of these soldiers, who were won over by the animal's intelligence, courage, cunning, endurance, and dignity in the face of death.

In Mongolia, horsemen used eagles to track wolves. In America, the Comanche caught them with lassos and killed them with spears. Just like bounty hunters, professionals hired by the governors of Colorado and other states tracked wolves to their lairs, where they exterminated the litters.

Today, the species is extinct in Ireland, the United Kingdom, France (the wolves that roam there came from Italy through the Alpine passes), Belgium, the Netherlands, Germany, Switzerland, Austria, and Hungary. And the hunt continues in Eastern Europe, Mongolia, China, and in the Balkans. It was only in 1979 that the Berne Convention finally declared *Canis lupus* to be a protected species.

The night was as black as pitch.

Jeff was away. I couldn't sleep, so I had thrown myself into working on a score. Harvey whined and scratched at the back door to go out. She had become quite used to our walks and considered them to be her due. I looked at my watch. It was two o'clock in the morning. Oh well, why not? I closed my book, and the two of us took off at a brisk pace, heading north. Like a yo-yo, my shadow stretched far out in front of me and then shrank, in rhythm with the yellow haloed streetlights. Everything in the neighborhood was asleep at that hour—people, cars, and dreams. Except for a few night birds and the far-off passing of a car, rushing to get back to home sweet home, no sound broke the general slumber, which was so complete as to seem narcotic.

I particularly liked walking in the middle of the night at a brisk pace, feeling my muscles ache and my hips swing, tracing in that movement invisible arabesques in the air. Often I imagined that I was going to keep going straight, taking long strides, without ever turning back, and without ever breaking the rhythm of my walk and its military tempo. I could walk for a long time, until I anesthetized the incredibly mechanical machine of my body, with its ferocious vitality. This had begun as a child, when I would hurt my hands. As an adult, I liked inflicting other ordeals on myself, like running, or climbing stairs as fast as I could while holding my breath. In hotels where I stayed when I was giving concerts, I would escape into lifting weights, running on treadmills, and trying out all those magnificent bodybuilding machines, on which I would exercise until my head swam. Transcending fatigue allowed me to access another level of movement, the level of thought, and then of music through rhythm, through tempo.

That night, while walking, I remember that I was thinking about *The Night of the Hunter,* the film directed by Charles Laughton, which I had rented several times in Paris while I was learning English. I had been astounded by the beauty of the scenes that show the two orphans drifting in their boat down the Mississippi. Do you remember the images of that troubling and mysterious night? Of all of the world's innocence wrapped up in the sleep of those children whose fate is in the hands of the river? And destiny in the shape of that immense, unpredictable river with its shifting islands, which I had a hard time imagining flowed only a few hundred miles from my new home. I liked the fact that, like Ulysses in his boat, Moses in his basket, and Romulus and Remus on the Tiber, Charles Laughton had decided to create his own founding myth, and that he had done so with film, the quintessentially American way of storytelling. The captainless ship slides between the two banks, where nature has posted its watchful animals—both victims and predators—on the lookout.

While walking, Harvey at my heels, I pictured the iguana, the owl, the spider, and the fox, all of those scenes in the film that I had particularly loved. I had the sensation that, now that I was in the uninhabited part of the neighborhood, the iguanas, owls, insects, and foxes on either side of the road were watching me pass by.

And it was at that instant that I saw it for the very first time.

The silhouette of a dog, but—with one glance, and despite the dark—one could instantly tell that it was not a dog. The animal had an indescribable walk—tense, furtive, as if it was making its way through a tunnel that was barely large enough. Its eyes had an almost supernatural glow. They gave off a muted light, violet and wild. Strangely, each step it took extinguished the sounds around it: no more night birds, no more slithering or rustling of wings, just a thick, tense silence. The creature looked at me, and a shiver ran through me—neither fear nor anxiety, just a shiver.

About twenty yards behind the animal, a tall man appeared in turn. Harvey gave off a little whimper and slipped off into the undergrowth, where she lay down. Alerted by the behavior of my dog, I froze.

"You often go out walking at this hour?"

The voice was harmonious, with a curious intonation that was devoid of both warmth and animosity. Despite the fact that I was alone in this deserted place at that hour, and despite the strangeness of the encounter, I did not feel as though I was in danger.

I answered in my very direct way, straight and to the point: "I'm a musician, a pianist, and sometimes I work late at night."

To tell the truth, it wasn't the man who intrigued me, it was his dog. In the dark, the animal looked strangely like Harvey. But it was radically different, not because of its shape, but rather because of its behavior. It kept its distance, somewhat apart. I had barely finished speaking when it approached me with an airy suppleness. It came up to sniff me, then immediately retreated.

"A musician, really?"

The stranger introduced himself. His name was Dennis. He loved classical music and owned a lot of records. I could come over when I liked. I found the approach a little direct, and I was amused at the idea of all the ploys a man is capable of to get a woman to come home with him. With a jerk of a thumb over his shoulder, he pointed out where he lived, and all at once I understood that this was the "cobra man." But what about the animal?

"It's a she-wolf," Dennis explained, before I could even ask the question.

At the same moment, she came toward me again. I didn't put out my hand.

"Don't move—she's shy."

I didn't budge, as if she wasn't there. Harvey stayed put, flattened to the ground. Dennis continued to talk, but I began to feel less at ease. My neighbors' warnings had done the trick: I remained on my guard. Musician? Thousands of records? Indeed, all he talked about was music. My doubts subsided when he mentioned a certain version of a work by Liszt played by Claudio Arrau, and Brahms's Third Symphony conducted by Karajan.

Let's see . . . Was he carrying the weapons that he supposedly owned? I examined his silhouette in the darkness. It was impossible to make out anything at all, except that he was about fifty and was very tall and thin. Occasionally, the lenses in his glasses shot little splinters of light into the night.

And then the she-wolf moved.

Slowly she approached me. My arms hung by my side. She came up to my left hand and sniffed it. I merely stretched out my fingers, and all by herself, she slid her head and then her shoulders under my palm. I felt a shooting spark, a shock, which ran through my entire body. The single point of contact radiated throughout my arm and chest, and filled me with gentleness. Only gentleness? Yes, but a most compelling gentleness, which awakened in me a mysterious singing, the call of an unknown, primeval force. At the same moment, the wolf seemed to soften, and she lay down on her side. She offered me her belly.

The minute she touched my hand, Dennis stopped talking. He

stared at the wolf. He seemed dumbstruck. When she lay on her side, he murmured: "I've never seen her do that."

"What?"

"Lie down like that. It's incredible for a wolf to do that, it's a sign of recognition and trust, even a sign of submission. Wolves have a real phobia of humans. They never lay themselves open like that if they don't feel safe. Even with me, she's never acted like that."

The wolf stayed at my feet. I had to struggle against a powerful urge to rub my face against her muzzle, to caress her and run with her into the night.

"How should I respond?"

I feared making a clumsy gesture, destroying with one inept movement this tacit, incredible, and unusual alliance that the wolf had made with me.

"Why don't you come pay her a visit, tomorrow or some other day? She's called Alawa."

I think that my happy smile could have lit up the night.

The society of wolves—the pack—is strangely similar to that of humans. It is, in effect, an animal version of democracy, an extremely strong-armed version, in which the leader, who is recognized as such by the others, dominates the others not by mere force or speed or hunting abilities, but in large part through psychological ascendancy; in this way, he ensures the survival of the group. In contrast to human society, observance of the rules is paramount.

In Europe, a pack consists of about a dozen animals, and in North America up to about thirty—a dominant male and his offspring, as well as several lone wolves who have come to swell the group. Within the pack, competition is severe. Nothing can be taken for granted, and certainly not one's place in the hierarchy. One has to know one's place, which animals are to be respected, and which animals must show their obedience. This law of submission, from the weakest to the strongest, and the acceptance of domination of leaders over those who are led, constitutes the very foundation of the pack.

Wolf pups learn this law as soon as they leave the den. The games they play, essentially simulations of future combat, teach them how to use their strength, their cunning, and their courage—qualities that later will determine their rank in the pack. The leader, which ethologists refer to as the alpha male, is the first to eat. He leads the hunt and the tracking of game. He wins the affection and absolute loyalty of the dominant female, who provides him with offspring. Only the alpha couple is allowed to procreate, which ensures that only the strongest genes are passed on. Nevertheless, the other wolves form couples that are just as faithful, but they will have no young as long as they are not dominant and have not founded their own pack. Many zoologists, ethologists, and biologists have examined this phenomenon and have dubbed it "psychological castration." However, they present no danger to the leader's litters: they are excellent surrogate parents, watching over the safety of the pups and feeding them regurgitated meat.

The wolf is a profoundly social animal and can live happily

only in the company of its fellow wolves. It establishes a very precise code of signals to confirm its place in the pack hierarchy. The tail, ears, and chops are used to express an animal's rank, but the facial expressions as well as various subtle body postures— hunching of the shoulders, bristling of the fur, flattening out, lying down on the side, the stomach, or the back—express what they are and what they want to be.

The German naturalist Daniel Schenkel was the first to study and set down the various expressions of this social language. He established a subtle distinction between postures that indicate the emotional state of each animal and, consequently, its place in the hierarchy. The animal's silhouette determines the status of each wolf: dominant or dominated.

For example, the leader, the alpha wolf, generally stands up quite straight, ears and tail erect, with his paws solidly planted. If he points his ears forward and bares his teeth, he is threatening, and the dominated wolves must show their allegiance by lowering their heads, jaws closed, tail between their legs.

And what about those who don't accept this rule? The uncontrollable ones, the rebels, the fighters? They must leave the pack and live alone, always circling around the group, looking for the chance to form their own pack or seeking a partner.

Dennis was not at all the person who had been described to me. Certainly, he was a real individual—a marginal character. As he had told me on the night of our first meeting, he ardently loved classical music and cultivated a real passion for nature and for the Great North. Sometimes, when I went to see him, he would tell me snippets of his life. I reconstructed it in segments, bit by bit. There was a lot missing, and often the various versions didn't match up. Which part was storytelling? Which parts of his rambling life, full of exaggeration but truthful? His origins were European. His mother was Russian and his father German. One day, several years after Dennis had died, I was giving a concert in Miami, and the whole day was filled with the premonition of a strange event. I had the feeling that I wasn't alone. A shadowy presence—sensed in the breeze that stirred the curtain of my dressing room, in the fall of my evening gown from its hanger—accompanied my every move. After the concert, a woman came to visit me backstage. I liked her immediately. She was eighty, but looked twenty years younger, since her body—thin, tall, straight—had kept its youthful suppleness. She wore a braided and tightly knotted chignon on her beautiful head, heavy with gray hair, and her piercing look could reach to the back of your neurological closet, from the attic of your dreams to the cellar of your schemes and petty-mindedness. She introduced herself: Dennis's mother. Immediately I knew the identity of my phantom.

That night, in my dressing room, the only night she came—the only night I met her—she didn't speak to me about music, or the program, or my playing. She talked to me for hours about the man of her life and the happiness he had given her, despite his extreme moods. Her gaze, which had been so firm, misted over, and I finally understood that she was talking not about a lover or a husband, but about her son. She talked to me about Dennis as if she were a woman in love, and even more than that, like a mother who was starstruck. She spoke of him as if he were still alive, as if he had never left her, and how could it be otherwise—does a son ever really leave his mother?

He had a sister as well. He described her as sophisticated. They had little in common. A Russian mother, a German father, and in the same breath, just when you were starting to get used to this exotic European lineage, he announced that his family was from the Bronx, and that he had worked in Canada, returning with a fascination for the north, the Great North. Sometimes he came across as a graduate of a top engineering school, other times as a soldier and Vietnam veteran. Each version had a ring of truth: The numerous plans that he could whip up for me with just a few pencil strokes, when I described for him the planned enclosures, the wolves, and the reserve, supported the thesis that he was an engineer. His weapons, that he had been in Vietnam. He really did have an arsenal, including several Kalashnikovs, which he had fun teaching me to shoot with. What did it matter? He had the air of a movie star from the 1940s, with a beautiful voice and an astonishing contrast between the precision of his gestures and his intense nearsightedness. He was incredibly charming—the charm of a beautiful friendship. Sometimes he would disappear for days on end. Where? Why? He never, upon his return, explained. I never asked. I often left Florida myself for concerts, and we told each other very little about our daily lives. When he was in a talkative mood, he would recall the beginning of his adventures with Alawa, his she-wolf.

He had always dreamed of having a wolf. The opportunity finally came during one of his diverse activities—this time, a scientific expedition to the Great North. There, he became friends with a biologist, who had presented him with a young she-wolf that had been taken from a litter. In Canada, wolf legislation is much less strict than in the United States.

And so Alawa had been living with him for nearly four years. Right from the start, Dennis had tried his best to socialize her—walks in the park, playing with children, all of it in vain. Alawa was a misanthrope. Like all members of her species, she considered the human being to be her sworn enemy, her tormentor, someone her genes and instincts had taught her to fear.

Even though her life as a pet and a city dweller had increased her fear, it had not dampened either her nature or her wildness. At Dennis's house, everything was destroyed. He had ended up giving over the ground floor of the house to her, where the furniture was lacerated, chewed, and broken. The prodigious strength of her jaws and her need to burn up her species' inexhaustible energy had crushed everything around her that could be crushed. The sofa cushions were gutted, their foam lacerated; the wood of the furniture was scraped, and the feet had been chewed to matchsticks. There was not an object or a single piece of furniture that was even remotely intact. It looked as if a bomb had hit it.

In the large backyard, Dennis had built an enclosure where Alawa paced back and forth for hours. Between the pen and the house, he had created a door. Alawa could not be left alone for long, and when Dennis left, she had to be shut up in the house.

The day after my visit, I rushed back to Dennis's house to see her again. I had talked about her to Jeff on the phone, my voice trembling with excitement.

"Anyone would think you were in love," he joked.

Yes, that was exactly it. I had fallen in love with this she-wolf, and my curiosity and my enthusiasm looked like passion. As on the first night, Alawa greeted me with all the signs of happiness. Dennis's astonishment never ceased to grow. This immediate understanding astounded him, and pleased me. That afternoon, all we talked about was *Canis lupus.* I was insatiable. Dennis interwove his conversation with memories of his experiences in Vietnam and lyrical flights about the Great North.

As night fell, I suddenly got up to leave.

"I haven't shown you my CDs. Can you come back tomorrow?"

For Alawa, I would have come back every day and stayed for hours on end. And in fact, that's just what I did: every day, I followed the path to the little house on the edge of the neighborhood in the deep woods.

As it turned out, Dennis did have a very nice collection of recordings and an excellent stereo system on the upper floor. Everything was under lock and key to prevent the wolf from getting in.

Outside of time set aside for music, I shared some very special happy moments with Alawa. The exchange of affection was strong and exuberant on her part. She would appear out of nowhere. Often she took me by surprise. Each time, Dennis decoded her gestures and told me how I should respond.

"I'm going to be away for a week."

"Oh?"

"I'll come back every evening to feed Alawa, but you can come see her during the day if you want."

Enter her territory alone? Was it dangerous? The question hung in the air, in the silence with which I greeted his offer. We looked at each other, and I knew that he didn't know the answer, or that a doubt still remained. I also understood that Dennis was putting me to the test. It was up to me to decide. Would I have the guts? The strength to not show the slightest fear?

Fifteen or twenty seconds later, we decided that the following morning, at dawn, Dennis would leave the house keys in a flower pot.

❦

Wolves reappeared on French soil in 1992, in the Mercantour National Park in the lower French Alps. They crossed the Italian border to settle in this Alpine zone. Today there are about thirty of them, protected under the Berne Convention, which France did not sign until 1990, eleven years after its ratification. Formerly, the French army was mobilized as soon as a wolf was spotted. This is because, in the summertime, *Canis lupus* attacks flocks of sheep grazing in mountain pastures. Thus, each year, about a thousand sheep fall into their clutches—which is nothing compared to the havoc wreaked by wild dogs.

In the past, these attacks were avoided by shepherds and their herd dogs, and by keeping the animals penned in at night. But international competition has forced farmers to keep their production costs down in order to stay competitive in the face of imported lamb from New Zealand and Argentina. Thus, they let their flocks wander alone in the mountains, where the wolf has established its territory. To punish the wolves and get rid of them, even though they know full well that the species is protected, some farmers shoot wolves or lace bits of meat with strychnine and cyanide, and they do so with complete impunity.

Will fear of the wolf seize Europe by the throat? Or is it just a typically French problem? In Italy and Spain (where some two thousand wolves have been counted), the presence of shepherds and their dogs help prevent losses. In Romania, for example, *Canis lupus* lives in harmony with humans, bears, sheep, and a great many other species.

Is it a coincidence that wild women and wolves share the same reputation? Clarissa Pinkola Estés has written about the strange similarities between the history of wolves and that of women, from the point of view of both work and passion. And it's true, wolves and women do share certain mental characteristics: sharpened senses, playfulness, and an extreme sense of devotion.

Above all, both wolves and women are treated with the same predatory violence, stemming from the same misunderstanding. Whether as sirens or witches, women were punished for their primitive, wild, and essential relationship to nature. There are those who would destroy the buried memory of the Garden, whose beauty and loss can bring to the surface both strange memories and powerful intuitions. Some women were burned, others banished. Still other women, when they run beneath the moon, see their shadows stretch and sway like the shadow of the she-wolf. They are the ones who laugh and love unreservedly, who give birth and create, who rejoice in their shapes and in the hot blood that issues from their bodies, and who know instinctively the properties of every herb and which fruits are poisonous.

They are the ones about whom the South American *cantadoras* sing "the woman who lives at the end of time" or "the woman who lives at the edge of the world." This woman, this wolf, is the friend and the mother of those who are lost, of those who need to understand, those with a riddle to solve, those who wander in the desert or the forest, seeking an answer, a sign, or a hope.

The next day, I found the flower pot without any trouble. I put the key in the lock and opened the door. Holding my breath, I listened.

If my intrusion had been noticed by the wolf, she didn't show it. Not a growl. I closed the door behind me, my heart beating.

"Alawa?"

She pounced on me like a huge weight. I was petrified. What should I do? How should I react? I listened intently to her short, panting breath. Was she growling? Does a wolf growl? Her teeth gleamed so close to my jugular that with one bite she could have slashed my throat.

However, she seemed not to notice my uncertainty. I focused on breathing gently. Slowly and very calmly, I put down my bag to take out a score. Finally, Alawa loosened her grip and pulled away in turn.

She sometimes had fun repeating this sudden, simulated attack. One day I was studying a score, and once again, although I hadn't heard the slightest sound or the smallest breath, she fell on me, her eyes fixed and gleaming, baring her teeth in a strange smile. I sometimes had the impression that she had sudden memories, brief flashbacks of her original wildness, and I wondered if all at once she would give in to this call, throw herself on me, tearing me to pieces and plunging her muzzle into my entrails. A few seconds later she would calm down and curl up at my feet.

After our first encounter, I came to see her often. She burst with joy on seeing me come through the door. We interacted, she biting my ears, pulling my hair, trying to drag me around, and working herself into a tizzy. Very quickly we understood each other; we got along. A blink of an eye, a movement of my hand, and she knew; she was there; she never left my side. When I played, she lay down at my feet, attentive, her muzzle on her paws, her tail waving like a metronome.

Emotionally, Alawa was one of the great presences of my life. Our mutual attachment and confidence were absolute. Dennis never ceased to marvel at it. A relationship with a she-wolf is almost impossible when you have not raised it yourself. The spontaneity of our connection was rare and inexplicable.

Alawa was from Canada, and her pelt was strange, with very long hair. Her eyes were an intense yellow, and with her I felt happy, whole, and absurdly young and strong.

I began to take her out of her pen, to take her with me far from Dennis's house. I had her cross the street, follow a path, and trot along with me through the woods, down by the swamp. I then wanted to bring her home, but at this, Jeff blew up.

My friendship with Dennis worried him. He was somewhat skeptical at my outings with Alawa. Was I out of my mind? Walking around with a wild animal, and a wolf at that, risking my life and the lives of our neighbors? Had I forgotten that it was completely illegal for Dennis to keep her?

I listened, determined not to give in. I agreed to nothing. I continued to take Alawa with me wherever I went.

There was mutual caution between Jeff and Alawa. Whenever he came near me, she shied away at first, her eye a bit crazy. Despite everything, Jeff finally understood that I would never give her up. So he looked the other way when I decided that we were going to move to a house that was much more isolated, in a very large park, so that Alawa could feel happy and at home, with space around her. Our new house was in a somewhat isolated zone on the edge of the woods and swampland. Sometimes I heard her howling at night, howling endlessly, modulating a powerful, vertical sound.

"Why is she howling like that? It makes my blood run cold," said Jeff, who had awoken with a start.

I answered him, my heart beating, seized by the desire to run and join her: "Alawa isn't howling, she's calling."

How could I tell him? That cry, it was as if the spirit of an animated, cheerful, and free woman were mounting and riding me; as if, inside me, something was moving, something whose hooves I felt sink into impenetrable forests, plunge through the snow of my soul, drive into my heart like the point of an arrow, the powerful nostalgia of an Elsewhere that was to come, the one that had haunted me as a child. Would he understand? I didn't think so, since I was incapable of explaining this exaltation even to myself. So I didn't tell him anything.

Alawa and I made countless trips between the two houses. When she was outside during the day, she was timid. She preferred going out at night. However, as soon as she knew she was at home, with me, she was perfectly calm and happy.

On Dennis's bookshelves I found several books about wolves. Ethology, zoology, environmental law. I started to leaf through them with a very specific idea in mind: to find a chapter that described in detail the animals' facial expressions and postures when they form a pack. I read everything. I devoured those pages because I was so fascinated by the subject. They talked about life in the pack, the social system among these animals, and especially their intelligence. A wolf in combat knows when it is beaten and must show submission; the victor will usually not keep up the attack or kill it. The wolf is a supremely social animal. I wiped away a tear while reading the story told by the naturalist Robert Hainard. He had personally watched as a wounded she-wolf, limping and very weak, dragged itself through the snow, while her companion stayed right by her side, feeding and protecting her.

I began to study ethology. I audited courses at the university, and I attended conferences. I traveled throughout America visiting wildlife reserves where specialists studied the biology and behavior of wolves. In a few months, I knew by heart the names of all the top specialists in the country. I rarely missed their lectures. I was especially interested in the courses given by Erich Klinghammer and those of David Mech. I studied ethology the way I studied music when I was young, intensely and with determination, for hours on end. I was fascinated by the subject, and the incredible space of freedom and independence to which it gave me access. I decided to adopt Alawa; I wanted to create a foundation and a park devoted entirely to the study and rehabilitation of *Canis lupus.*

It was inevitable that my musical work slowed during these studies and trips. I continued to explore the same repertoire, without expanding it, in order to devote myself to my new work. I focused my attention on chamber music, but when I did give myself to music, I did so with an entirely dedicated spirit and one hundred percent of my energy.

I made dozens of appointments with American governmental authorities, in order to obtain the necessary permissions to create and operate the foundation and to keep the wolves. With each official I met, I had to prove my worth. I set aside all the earnings from my concerts to buy property where I could install my pack.

My passion and enthusiasm were unshakable; I would have moved mountains to get what I wanted. The time of doubts, abysses, and cracks had come to an end. A primal force carried me, lifted me up, and took me much further than I ever could have imagined. And yet, I felt very guilty about Alawa. Between my concerts and my travels, I spent very little time in Tallahassee.

The she-wolf went back to Dennis's house. I knew that she was miserable in my absence. I missed her, too—terribly. I consoled myself by repeating that very soon, she would be with me, among her own kind in a space worthy of her, where she would have a role to play. This idyllic vision did not always quiet my sorrow.

It is impossible today to list precisely how many traps and poisons humans have invented to exterminate wolves, but the ingenuity and the cruelty of their devices reveal the barbarism that went into killing the beast. For example, certain wolf traps consisted of four sets of steel teeth, held in place by a spring triggered when the bait was taken. The trap then immediately sprang open inside the wolf's jaws, spreading them wide as it hoisted up the animal to leave it dangling by its head.

Traps hidden beneath cut branches opened onto pits bristling with stakes, sharpened spikes, or barbed blades. Nets closed around wolves, hanging them upside down. Snares would strangle them. Meat was hidden at the end of a box, whose entrance was equipped with a vertical or horizontal guillotine. Or meat was laced with a veritable arsenal of horrors: hooks that would lacerate their throats, ground glass, pellets of arsenic and strychnine, and needles. One of the traps consisted of coiling a long, thin, extremely sharp wire inside a piece of meat. Once ingested, the coil sprang open, shredding the animal's insides and causing a slow, agonizing death.

And then Jeff and I separated, and I left for New York. One morning I arrived on Fifth Avenue, ready to make a fresh start. On a whim. Alone. Determined to put some distance between Florida and myself, and to never look back, so as not to be turned into a pillar of salt. I had decided to found the center in a region somewhere north of the city.

I had nevertheless abandoned the idea of the wide open spaces of Canada: my profession required that I live near an airport. I would start my search from this city, where most of the real estate agencies were located.

Nothing prepares you for New York as a whole, or for the Bronx, or Harlem, or Manhattan, or Staten Island, not even for Times Square: nothing and no one can prepare you for the shock of this city, our world's true center of gravity. When you touch down there, or go up there, you change universes. New York is a challenge to our very concept of a city. Everything there is different—flat spaces, blocks, reliefs, proportions, placement of lighting, number, measure, weight, symmetrical effects, vertical and horizontal forces—the scale has changed. The straight, infinite lines of the building fronts make them seem as ethereal as they are inhuman. They are like an answer to the lesson of Icarus: as if one had wanted to hoist them up to the heavens, from where you would never fall. Maximum current, perpetual high voltage, a persistent high-pressure zone. New York is a place where the first movement is one of anxiety: so many stressed people—hundreds, thousands, millions— dashing through the streets, whose only purpose seems to be to keep the city going. No social connections, no friendliness. There, you don't feel the weight of history or of what is to come: everything is in the here and now, in a permanent, futureless present. Every minute is different, nothing ever repeats, and everything seems absolutely new. You can hear every language spoken on every street-corner, and you can see every type of person, from the eccentric poet to the stressed-out CEO. There, you can witness every type of sin—from the biggest to the most cowardly—connected to money.

Above all, you understand what it means to be alone in the middle of a crowd. You live with a premonition of catastrophe, but an elated premonition, hanging at the edge of madness.

One day when I was out walking, I heard the cries of a woman being beaten somewhere on the upper floor of a building, while two children furtively made a drug deal, and at the same moment—in the middle of the screams and the drugs—a huge limousine, long and white, the kind you see only in New York, with six doors and tinted windows, rolled by in the silence of a finely tuned engine. All around, not a tree, not a field, but a basketball court covered with asphalt right up to the edge. At that moment I knew that this city was indeed that of the Prince of this World, the place of every vice where money flows freely. I knew that New York was where souls were lost; I finally understood the origin of those little wisps of white smoke that rose from the pavement all year round: hell was right beneath our feet.

At first I liked this gigantic chaos. New York forces you to reconsider the order of things, in an intoxication that can make your head spin. It matched my inner turbulence, and the electric energy that the city gave off was equal to my determination. I wanted to blend into a place that would remain utterly foreign to me, one that would neither influence my imagination nor soften me. I wanted to toughen myself up, temper my temperament. I continued to inflict a draconian regimen on myself so that I didn't touch my capital, stretching each dollar as far as it would go to feed myself: I wolfed down a hot pretzel that I bought at a street corner, and a very hearty soup from a deli in the Bronx.

I didn't wander endlessly around in New York as I had done

when I first arrived in Paris. I crisscrossed the city, directory in hand, visiting various administrative offices and seeking out laundromats where I could wash the single change of clothes I had with me, aside from what I wore for my concerts. In New York, washing machines are usually found in the basements of apartment buildings. The places I lived in were too poor to have such a luxury.

Over a period of three years—I didn't move to South Salem, New York, until the spring of 1997—I moved an average of once every three months, without telling anyone, especially not my parents, from whom I successfully concealed my voluntary poverty. I hardly ever unpacked my little suitcase: it served as a closet. Renting a place in New York was very difficult for me at that time. I didn't have a bank account there, or a green card—legally, I didn't need one, since I returned on average once a month to play in Europe and thus always spent less than the maximum time allowed by a work visa in the States. Here, no one knew me. I was a complete stranger. At any rate, classical musicians are anonymous there, unless you happen to be Luciano Pavarotti or Yo-Yo Ma.

At the time, I had played in New York only twice, not nearly enough for people to remember my name—I'm not talking here about celebrity, or even simple credibility. In fact, it was hellish trying to live there, with your only legal status being a work visa. Managing to rent a pied-à-terre was a real feat, and I often found myself in indescribable squats. Not because I wanted to, but because I didn't have any other choice. Over thirty-six months I changed my address fifteen times. The places I lived had one thing in common: they were located in squalid, disreputable areas. My neighbors were people who screamed, beat each other, and drank. I moved so often for the simple reason that the landlords required a bank guarantee—which I didn't have—for rental periods longer than three months. So as soon as I moved into a new place, I set off in search of the next one, and at the same time I visited properties where I would finally be able to build the center and move Alawa in.

It was thus that I landed in Alphabet City, on Manhattan's Lower East Side, in the middle of a neighborhood that was largely black and Hispanic. Drugs were sold under my windows, and across the street was a café where people got drunk and screamed. I lived in a studio the size of a shoe box.

One night in this studio, I was looking for something in a closet and I suddenly had a vision of chains and locks. For a moment I was surprised; I didn't understand what they meant, until the day I discovered—when visiting the first enclosure that I had built for the wolves—that the entrance gate, chain, and lock were exactly the same as those I had seen in my waking vision. Nevertheless, at the time I didn't allow myself to even daydream about enclosures: I had barely enough money to live.

In Alphabet City, I was taken in by a gay couple. One of them was Cuban, and the other was flamboyant. He had a body like Adonis's, with glowing skin, and he wore shorts and Rollerblades in every season, even when it was snowing or raining. I still remember the photos on the mantel of him and his companion wearing nothing but Hawaiian leis. I stood there speechless! At least they were genuinely friendly, unlike those who talked about a love of humanity, compassion, brotherhood, and all sorts of fine sentiments, but who in the end created incredible hassles about everything to do with the apartment: the refrigerator, the stove, the rent, the keys, and the times to come in and go out. Today, these are the people who would have you believe that I'm their best friend and who come to see me every time I give a concert in New York.

My working conditions had never been more difficult, for the simple reason that I had no piano. And things would not have been any simpler if I had had one, since I moved so frequently.

And yet I was never seized by doubt, as would happen in Paris before my departure and during those singular days at La Roque d'Anthéron. I had one idea in mind. This goal—an enclosure where I could protect wolves and defend their cause—carried me along, with the force of a tidal wave. It swept away all the details of piano work. I had finally decided not to become a slave to the instrument.

I had become a wild woman.

I resigned myself to it. Whenever I was gnawed by the desire to play or to put my study of a piece into practice, and there was no piano near at hand, I told myself that the only important thing in music is the discourse: the vehicle is incidental. I have a theory: *Whoever can do the most can also do the least.* It is so rare to find a magnificent piano, one that is exactly to your liking, that if by some miracle you do find one, you run the risk of being easily disappointed when playing some other, lesser instrument. But if you work only with a mediocre piano, all you need is to find a good one for a concert and you're in seventh heaven.

Plus, when I wanted to work, I went to the Steinway building on Fifty-seventh Street, or I would rent a piano for two or three hours. (Sometimes more, but rarely: it was ruinously expensive.)

In fact, I had never rehearsed so much in my head. And with my heart, without using my hands.

Between 1990 and 1995, I managed to break all my ties with Paris. I continued to go regularly to Aix, and the music business, which was benevolent when I was just starting out, forgot about me. I fell back into a delicious anonymity—I had other projects, other storms raging in my head, which two trips to Paris didn't help with.

My life at the time was an isolated one. I was very taken up by music, even if I was at the keyboard very little. I worked using thought, image associations, mental projections, and visions of architecture—of colors. I let it distill. It wasn't until 1997 that I rented my first upright piano. In Florida, I would go to the university. In New York, I would go to Steinway or elsewhere, to friends' places if necessary, but only when I needed to be face-to-face with the instrument so that the sensed conception could manifest.

I became the owner of my first concert piano, a Steinway D, only in 2001. I acquired it thanks to Serge Poulain, a brilliant technician of the Berlin Steinway-Haus. It was one of the fleet of concert pianos, not those for private individuals. A young piano, magnificent, recently out of the factory. And Steinway had the kindness to deliver it, wrapped, from Berlin to my home.

I had the wolves. I had music.

I had the music of the wolves under the moon, and my playing held the animality that safeguards the artist.

❧

In 1994, a pack of wolves was reintroduced into Yellowstone Park, where the last herds of bison and elk flourish; the last Yellowstone wolf had been killed in 1924. These fourteen wild wolves had been captured in the Canadian Rockies by scientists from the Gray Wolf Recovery Project, and released in this magnificent territory devoted to native American wildlife. The fourteen wolves formed three packs. The following year, sixteen wolves that had been captured in British Columbia arrived to swell the ranks and to reestablish the balance between the herds of herbivores that flourished there. (Of these, the wolves only attack and eat sick or old herd members, thus ensuring a precious balance between species and preservation of flora.) At the top of the pyramid of predators, the wolf holds the job of head biodiversity engineer. The remains of its hunting expeditions provide nourishment for an entire chain of species, birds, insects, etc. This chain plays an extremely important role in the regeneration of plant and animal life. Thus, the reintroduction of the wolves into Yellowstone allowed scientists to measure their impact on the ecosystem. In two years, their presence cut the coyote population in half and, as a result, doubled the population of rodents hunted by eagles and falcons, which came back to these lands from which they had virtually disappeared.

In the same period, from Montana to Minnesota, in places where it had never completely disappeared, the wolf resettled its former territories, following wild trails that had remained in collective memory. And what a return! Although there are still some 60,000 wolves in Canada, there were barely 2,500 in Minnesota, on the other side of the border. Now they are making their way into Wisconsin and Michigan, and farther south and west toward Utah. Nothing can stop them, not even the wealth of game on their territory, as in Yellowstone.

The U.S. Department of Agriculture keeps an eye on the packs, as well as on individual wolves that go off to live farther afield than the authorities would like. In 1995, a young wolf couple captured in Canada were released in Idaho; soon after, they were found devouring a heifer ninety miles away. The female was captured and brought back to its original territory, but the male managed to get away. A few weeks later, the female rejoined the male, and the pair began indulging in forbidden feasts once again.

Every researcher and biologist who has monitored wolves agrees: no other animal is more fascinating. And even if they observe the pack only from time to time, they all end up becoming attached to one of its members, giving it a name, now and again trying to exchange glances and signals.

I particularly remember Atka, born in Minnesota of Jack and Thelma, two arctic wolves. This pup was barely a week old when he arrived at the center, and he didn't hesitate even a second before gulping down a baby bottle of milk. Later the veterinarian would enrich his milk with an egg, cream of rice, and ground meat.

There was something splendid in watching him feed, his enormous paws placed on the bottle, in seeing his ears prick up, trembling, at the sound of the howling of the pack, which frolicked just a hundred meters from his den.

For two months, Atka ("guardian angel" in Inuit) stayed in the "nursery," and then I took him into the principal enclosure to make the acquaintance of Apache, Kaila, and Lukas. A couple of months later, we did it again, this time for good. We brought Atka into the main enclosure, face-to-face with his fellow wolves. After respectfully waiting his turn to eat the remains of a quarter of a deer, Atka played with Lukas.

All the social gestures, all the postures signaling the authority of one and the submission of the other were used. The center had invited a school group to watch this encounter. The children had remained quietly behind the enclosure fence, carefully watched over by the accompanying adults. Then they left to get back on their bus.

Alone, his hands gripping the steel chain-link fence, one child didn't move. He didn't take his eyes off the two wolves playing. His group was gradually moving away.

He watched and smiled serenely. Finally, he clapped his hands, happy, magnificently happy.

"Thank you," said one of the adults who had come back to fetch him. "This is the first time this child has come out of his silence and apathy."

She had tears in her eyes.

The child, like his entire group, was autistic.

Today, when I play, I no longer feel that I am alone. I have the feeling of a visitation. What a pianist does by his or her work is to prepare the moment of this visitation. When I cross the stage, I am alone, but as soon as I begin to play, I am not. I am protected by a presence. Is it the presence of music? Or of the composers whose works I am playing?

I prefer the second hypothesis: I've played Brahms and Beethoven so much that I feel as though I know them intimately, as if they were with me, as if they were prompting me. There is a *sforzando* passage in *The Tempest*: at that point, I can't get it out of my head that Beethoven makes a movement with his elbow, that he must have made such a movement, and that he will continue to do so for eternity. For me, the image of Beethoven is that of a snorting horse shaking its head—even if that means nothing to other people. As for Brahms, for some strange reason, I see him leaning slightly forward, but I don't know if this leaning is due to anticipation, contemplation, or perplexity. Each time this is a physical image. In addition, when I step outside myself and watch myself as I'm playing, sometimes I see a light come down that envelops the entire piano. I know that they are that light. At that instant, I know that I am there to receive this heavenly song and, inasmuch as I am its vehicle, to conduct this gentle lightning bolt of love through the core of the tree to the center of the earth, the heart of the earth, this throbbing star.

❧

Day after day, whenever I had a few hours free, I struggled to find the right place for the wolf project. I won't go into the details or how I did it, or the mountains of red tape and permits—it was both tiresome and trying. But I will never forget my joy the day the real estate agent called me. He had finally found my paradise.

"It's out of your price range, but no one wants it for the moment. The owners can't find a buyer; if you make an offer, they might accept."

The agent and I took the train up to visit the place. February had covered the countryside with a thick blanket of snow. As we left New York behind, I was struck by the beauty of the landscape. It was stark, enchanting, bathed in the flickering light of the aurora borealis. It was wild and silent. It was Elsewhere, that Elsewhere I had always hoped for.

After we spent more than an hour on the train, the owners were waiting for us at the station. I spoke little going there in the car; I was absorbed by the splendor of the landscape. There was no one around. No houses. The frozen stretches glinted with thousands of diamonds. I imagined Alawa running here, leaping through the snow in huge bounds, and rushing down the hills. Finally, we stopped by the side of a small, completely uninteresting house, and I understood why, despite the surrounding countryside and the size of the property, no one had wanted this drab, isolated place, far from everyone and everything. My heart leaped for joy.

This house was just the ticket. I named my price and we closed the deal.

For six months, having finally received the necessary permits from the state authorities, I had to relandscape the terrain and enclose it with fences deeply set in the ground and topped with overhang wire. A horde of volunteers from the community came to help me with the work. And what a lot of work it was! We had to landscape the slopes to accommodate the wolves, and create well-sheltered hollows where they could build their dens; security cameras had to be installed to survey the safety of the enclosure. We worked like beasts, pushing wheelbarrows, carting away dirt with the workers, planting saplings. But I was flying. Right from the start, I felt happy. I knew that I had finally reached my port.

The Wolf Conservation Center was born. Today some thirty people work there. We were able to house the first ambassador wolves in the preserve, fed on deer meat; we made sure that the place where we left the meat changed every day. Today, Kaila, Apache, Lukas, and Atka live there, and they have given me the best reason to return to the piano; they have furnished me with a fresh and vital impetus. Kaila was the first she-wolf I saved and settled in the camp. Dennis had recommended that I call the first she-wolf by this name, to pay tribute to the Inuit, from the northern part of America, who have a legend about Kaila, the supreme spirit of the sky.

According to the legend, the Adam and the Eve of the Inuit are bored. Eve speaks to Kaila: "We are all alone, and we are bored." "Make a hole in the ice and see what you pull out," said Kaila. From the hole, the woman pulls animals, including a caribou. "I have given you a beautiful gift with this caribou. Thanks to it, your people will prosper," said Kaila. And the people do prosper because of the caribou. The men go hunting, and in order to bring back the most handsome trophies, they kill the most beautiful caribous. One day, the only caribous left are sick, old, or thin. Their future looks bleak. So the woman returns to see Kaila to complain. "Make another hole in the ice and see what you pull out."

This time, a wolf emerges. Once released, the wolf attacks the sick animals and leaves the healthy ones alive. The troop of caribou regenerates. And thus ends the Inuit legend of Kaila and the wolf.

Currently, one of my greatest pleasures is to go and work on my music with them, in the enclosure, at night. When I enter their territory, I never adopt the posture of a conqueror. I am careful to show respect to avoid a hierarchical conflict with the alpha male. He is the one I approach first. He greets me, standing, tail slightly erect, ears pointed forward. As soon as he allows it, the others come to greet and kiss me. If I were to allow them, they would nibble the corner of my lips the way they gently bite each other's chops, as a sign of affection. After several minutes of commotion, the wolves settle down and surround me. They lay down around me, in a choreography that is always harmonious, and with such elegance you would think it was orchestrated. Then I can begin to mentally work on my scores.

Here, in my American refuge, there is something harsh that I love, the snow, the storm. I rehearse Beethoven's *Tempest* with an awareness of the power on the other side of the door. In winter, I have the bite of the cold and the howling of the wind that destroys and rebuilds; the cosmos leans in against my little house. In these magic moments, I practice the piano with an incomparable happiness. I become a sorceress, a medium. In a splendid freedom, music fulfills me, brings me into those spaces where I stride swiftly in, places that inhabit me in turn, and with them, the memory of all those whom I love and admire.

I like to laugh, absurdly and with my entire body, for hours on end. On the other hand, I lack the capacity to cry very much. I regret this: sometimes the sorrow I hold inside jolts me. I feel it rising in my chest, enormous and powerful, and I know that it's going to completely take over my thoughts. The trigger is always the same: the idea of loss. The first time I felt this definitive loss, and cried without being able to stop—intensive cathartic tears, followed by serene ones, long, hot tears that connect you with the very base of yourself—was after having played Brahms's First Concerto for the first time in concert. I succumbed to these tears several hours later, on the plane that was taking me to a recital in another city. I was seated up front, facing the gray partition that divides the sections of seats, next to the window. It was night; the seats were blue with red stripes. I put my forehead on the glass and I cried and cried. The passengers who could see me were perplexed, even embarrassed, but I did not try to hide my tears. Tears offered me a delicious liberation from the incredible tension of the concert, from the sorrow that Brahms expressed so well, a sorrow that can strangle and suffocate you.

I have never cried while playing, except on the night of September 11, 2001. Then, the tears wet my keyboard while I was playing Beethoven's Fourth Concerto, with the Orchestre de Paris under the baton of Christophe Eschenbach. It was at the Royal Albert Hall in London. And I cried again in the same place two years later, after having played Bela Bartók's Third Concerto. In the second part of the concert, John Adams presented the premiere performance of his *On the Transmigration of Souls,* composed in commemoration of 9/11, in front of an audience on its feet, overcome with emotion. All at once, the memories of that tragic day came back to me.

We had learned about the tragedy that afternoon, during rehearsal. Like everyone else, we ran to the television screens to attempt to grasp the unbelievable: this blind, mass murder, planned and thought out in advance, endlessly replayed in images; those bodies—lives, hopes, loves, and joys—that the terrible fire had forced into the void. Tiny silhouettes clinging to the twisted steel that had been their glory, as to the prow of a sinking ship. Already in another world—on the threshold of an inexorable farewell—their hands reaching out to us and, as if we might not see or hear them, waving their handkerchiefs and scarves at us while we stood powerless and numb with horror and fright, powerless, horribly powerless to save them. We were live witnesses to the creation of hell—not the place of sorrow, but the place where suffering is inflicted, where eternal suffering is invented.

We all asked ourselves whether—as a sign of mourning, as an expression of our despair and our compassion for these lives sunk into the pages of horror written in History's hand—we should cancel the concert planned for that very evening. Was it indecent to play after this barbaric act? While, on the other side of the Atlantic, the ruins of the World Trade Center still burned? Did Beethoven still have a meaning? Or music in its divine transcendence? And beauty? And being here? And going on? Can one play after Evil, Evil that is not like an illness but like drunkenness, "the drunkenness of an evil that Evil inspires"?

But then should we just stop everything? Put a gag on music, the very music that fundamentalism forbids?

At the risk of playing to empty seats, and in spite of all of our grief, we decided to hold the concert. And as if they had all come to the same conclusion, the audience came. That evening the hall was full. Full and silent, filled with a terrible silence—the silence of ghosts.

Before going onstage, I thought about New York, in the shadow in which I now lived, of its streets and avenues that I would so often take, of that day that had dawned in the glorious light of a September sun. Of the loss of those lives, and the loss of a certain innocence. I had a lump in my throat when I walked onstage, and when I greeted the audience and the musicians. All of them, I knew, had the same images in their minds, the same pain. But we played, played in honor of life.

From the very first measures, I felt a warm liquid dampening my hands and the keyboard—my tears.

I believe that the entire audience was crying as well.

The piano is an incomparable instrument when it is touched by a musician in whom nothing of the pianist remains. Then, it is music's most beautiful tool; the musician infuses it with his own song. At the keyboard, the invoked music emerges: the musical outline takes on color and wings. It is a vibrant reading of the spirit, resonant in its senses, touched by the heart. In this respect, there are two pianists—among many others, including Rubinstein, Horowitz, Arrau, Yudina, and Argerich—who have left their mark on me. Two rivals: Glenn Gould and Sviatoslav Richter.

Enough has been written about Glenn Gould to fill a library. Nothing has been left untouched: his madness, his sleepless nights, his childish laugh, his anxiety, his frailty coupled with an incredible strength, his hands that tremble, straighten, attack, and triumph—his El Greco hands, an extension of faith stronger than pain. People have talked about his body, pushed to extremes, and have listed his failures, his successes, his constant struggle—a struggle against himself as well. His resolute attention, the feeling of having faced danger: accepted, inevitable; the seriousness with which the intensity of the music leaves its mark on deep souls— his solitude, city to city, country to country, without friends, without lovers, but with friends by the thousands, and many lovers ... women briefly glimpsed ... desperate music lovers ... hysterical female admirers. Illness, disciples, rivals, the feeling of being about to leave, of leaving everything, of forgetting everything, of playing oneself. Then the speed, the oblivion, the worry ... no time to stop, no time to breathe, *presto*, forging ahead, even faster, the desire to prematurely reach the end, this impatience to see oneself, to hear oneself, to be taken out of oneself in the most intense music. And finally, the solitude. Everything that gave me the delightful impression that I had a musical older brother.

I have always been moved and disturbed by the idea that Gould's life ended the day after his fiftieth birthday, after having recorded an unforgettable version of Bach's *Goldberg Variations*, which was also his first record. I see in this a sign from heaven; thus the circle was closed, and Gould found fulfillment in his exemplary loyalty to Bach: that of the creature to the creator.

He loves being free. He believes passionately in what he plays, and he enjoys it. His music is truth that has proof: it believes and inspires belief in it. This mystery called incarnation. The music of Bach gives birth to Gould on earth, just as Gould raises it to the heavens. He has no need for the critics' truth: they can keep it. He lives at the core of what he interprets, and he plays that way that others pray. He calls upon his God, driven to despair if he does not find him. Fulfillment is all that he requires—this faith borders on a miracle.

With his Zen monk's head, his air of having seen it all before, Richter is admittedly different: in him, I see a man from Elsewhere. A traveler, in the sense that Schubert gave this word in his *Winterreise*: a pilgrim who crossed heaven and hell, but who does not stop there. He absolutely does not lend a "modern" cast to some early music: he gives ultramodern music—whose vital urgency we are only now beginning to hear—a background of eternity, in a world destined for self-destruction. He does not put the notes next to each other: it is the notes that line themselves up, on a higher, more compelling plane, summoned by a distilled emotion driven by intelligence. Whatever he does, the name of his art is depth, beneath the radiant layer of a formidable serenity. There, all is conceived, just as it is explained. Sviatoslav Richter gives only the appearance of perfect passion, this knowledge that is far beyond the perfection of desire. According to him, it is not this wind alone that rids the world of its imperfections, creating a whirlwind, circling an obsession. I see in it the magical movement of contemplation, the pace of ecstasy, this revolution that carries everyone along in the awe of a final vision.

My career as a pianist had at last found its path, and I had found my own unique sound. The real professional takeoff took place. I traveled a great deal. Concert and recital organizers put my name in their programs and on the posters of the most prestigious concert halls. Piano festivals clamored for my presence. The one at La Roque d'Anthéron—for so long my dream—honored me by having me play on the opening night of its 2002 program.

I worked with the greatest conductors on earth, of whom Kurt Sanderling will always be my favorite. Under his baton, I reached, as I rarely do, moments of intense communion with the music, the orchestra, and the work. One night in April 1999 in Paris, I wanted to cancel the next day's concert because the previous day I had had the feeling that it could all fall apart: we had accomplished the essential. I was convinced that under his direction I had played exactly as I should have, which is a very rare thing. After the joy of having done something so successfully, the following days are always intimidating, full of sadness, grieving those moments of beauty, glimpsed and just as quickly fleeting.

For this reason, I have never liked to run through a work before a performance. Why, for this first kiss, should one settle for less than ideal conditions? Bad hall, bad acoustics, a middling piano? The first time I refused to play a rehearsal concert, everyone had a fit.

"It's far too risky! You're crazy! You have to test your playing, evaluate your effects before facing the public. You're going to wreck your career."

I didn't give an inch, astonished each time at running into such general skepticism.

"This idea of trying out a work in advance is really ridiculous," Martha Argerich said to me one day. "The first time you play something is when you really need to be up to the task of what you imagined during hours of work, preparation and rehearsal."

I could have hugged her! It was so simple! When, more than this first time, is one more in need of a good hall, a good piano, a good conductor, and good acoustics? Imagine a first date, for which you prepared for hours and days, taking place in an ugly setting, and you looking wild and disheveled. It's unthinkable, isn't it?

In fact, if all of the conditions for excellence come together, this first time is not frightening; everything becomes more difficult the more you play a piece—the second time is dreadful.

The first time is often magic: nothing has happened to disturb your utopian vision of the work. Your playing is bathed in a fleeting, magnificent grace. The second time, you have to work yourself back up, start anew, just like that, with the awareness of everything that can happen. "One only knows a work completely when one has erred at every possible place," said Yehudi Menuhin.

As an illustration of this escalation of difficulties and the doubt that torments you more and more frequently, I will always remember one of the last concerts I gave under the direction of Kurt Sanderling.

It was in Munich. He was in the dressing room. I knocked at his door fifteen minutes before the start of the concert. He offered me a seat. We had a little time in front of us. I waited. He said nothing. He lifted his gaze to me. I waited some more.

"I have no idea, Hélène."

I felt my blood run cold.

"What do you mean, you have no idea?"

"You don't realize how difficult it is."

His voice was broken, terribly weary.

"At your age, you don't understand, you can't understand until you are my age, when you have seen how difficult things are in the long run. You only learn with experience. At your age, you haven't experienced enough arduous concerts to know how complicated and painful it can be."

He looked at me again, and all of the world's distress was in his gaze. I went back to my dressing room. He was abandoning me! My stomach clenched with undeniable terror, but two minutes before going onstage, I told myself: It's good, it's a good sign. You're going to have to surpass yourself, to find the rhythm on your own. Take it as a challenge and meet it.

Kurt Sanderling was completely right. The more time that goes by, the more playing becomes perilous. Of course, there are works that become practically organic for certain performers, the way Brahms's First Concerto is for me. And then there are others, like the concerto by Schumann, that intrigue you all the more, the more you play them. They have this particularly elusive quality, this mystery that makes them unique, but which mystifies you constantly, an indefinable something that is never really there, and is so difficult to convert into emotion, to do justice to. Everything depends on the works, on the personal relationship each artist has with these works, but at the base, yes, the more that time goes by, the more I understand just how much playing is a high-wire act.

❧

Very quickly as a child, I discovered music, the piano, and the work. Very quickly, I made Schumann's and Brahms's excesses my own. All of this lacked a dimension, or rather a latitude and a longitude. I had just found them and was finally at home, in a place in which language is created. Nature is also that—an enormous place where music germinates, music that is the other verb, the incubation of music in the song of the birds, the murmur of the wind in the giant elm trees, and at night, the howl of the wolves that call to me beneath the moon and sometimes give me the urge to run and plunge into the snow with them.

So I go out. I like spending time outdoors at night. I listen with all my might to the noises of water and fire. These noises have a parallel life, a rhythm, an ebb and flow with which I penetrate my own soul. One day I gave a piece of advice to a young musician in a master class. He had a problem balancing tension and relaxation;

he didn't understand how important ebb and flow were within the musical phrase. I told him: "You have to hear the sounds of nature, the rivers, the rain, and the birds."

Perhaps every privilege has its price, I don't know. Music gave me the chance to be able to make that sidestep that took me out of the daily routine, which was so deadly for me.

What can I tell you? At one moment in my life, my otherness was so intolerable to me that I no longer wanted to be myself. I got past this stage as well. I prefer taking the risk of disappointing people rather than lying to them. The goal in life is not to protect oneself; risk is part of the human condition. When all is said and done, I hope that a balance exists: if some are inevitably disappointed, others are happy. These situations always sadden me, but they no longer make me angry.

Little by little, I acquired this internal harmony as I accepted my contradictions and understood that certain beings are not a whole, but a jigsaw puzzle of contradictory hopes, and that it is suicidal, and even mutilating, to renounce one of these pieces under the pretext of wanting to look like a norm imposed by a model. But which model? That's the question—the model of the perfect little girl, of the polite young woman who marries the perfect son-in-law and reproduces the model in two or three children, or the model of the ethereal pianist? Each being carries the mystery of his or her contradictions, of his or her internal struggles.

We are all mysteries incarnate.

Today, I feel marvelously happy, because I have found my equilibrium, I have solved this problem of symmetry that, as a child, drove me to injure myself. I have found my secret coordinates—

personal and intimate—located between the wolves, the wildest form of nature, and the most refined music, between heaven and earth. I am in a state of permanent thankfulness. The only question that haunts me is how to give, to restore to others this same experience? It is my responsibility. This feeling of mission developed as soon as I moved to South Salem in 1997. When the wolves appeared. They were the link that connected me to the world. They allowed me to grow.

Alawa died in 1994, a few months before Dennis was found lifeless in his bed, no doubt as a result of a heart attack. For weeks in New York, their memory haunted me. I wandered the streets in tears. With Alawa dead, what was the good of the center? With Dennis gone, who would get excited about my projects? Who would cheer me up, encourage me, offer me advice over the telephone? And then, one of our telephone conversations came back to me. One day when I was in doubt, worn out by my daily struggles, crushed by the entire weight of the city, I called Dennis, ready to give it all up.

"Whatever doubts are eating at you, you must have known what you were doing when you left Florida. There must be a profound reason, much stronger than a few hiccups along the way. You have good instincts, Hélène. Find that reason. And if you can't find it, create it."

I created it. In 1999, we welcomed 750 children to the center; three years later, 8,500 of them came. Today we reach 20,000 yearly.

My greatest reward is the joy of these children when I put them in contact with the part of them that is the wolf—their freedom to choose freedom, to make that sidestep, to allow their being in its uniqueness to choose itself. This unique being that lives inside them like a shell at the bottom of the sea, a fertile seed in warm earth, before the world dries it out. Dries it out and dries out the rich soil with it, transforming it into sterile sand, the very sand that is used to measure time.

What would I like to transmit to them? Just as the wolf owns the land, and the fish the sea, as the bird owns the skies, and the gods own fire, humans beings must find their element, the fifth element, the only element from which we will never be excluded— our ability to make a difference. Art is part of this element, without which we wander aimlessly, orphaned and unhappy for our entire lives; without which we cut ourselves off from nature and the cosmos, because we become deaf, blind, insensitive, and desensitized.

I would like to help children recognize this space, their space, their chance to find themselves and positively affect the world around them and the lives of others, the space that the wolves showed me, this part of oneself that possesses the universe and, with it, time, through the key of music.

The space of essential health.